A GUIDE TO SHANGHAI

A GUIDE TO SHANGHAI

Joint Publishing Co.
Hong Kong 1984

Compiled by
Zhang Wei'e
Wu Li
Translated by
Cheng Runming
Zhan Yunzhao
Translation Editors
Chan Chiu Ming
Ho Kai

Copublished by
Joint Publishing Co. (HK)
9 Queen Victoria Street, Hongkong
and
Shanghai Scientific and Technical Publishers
450 Ruijin Erlu, Shanghai

Printed in Hongkong by
L. Rex Offset Printing Co., Ltd.
14/F., No. 4, Yip Fat St., Aberdeen, Hongkong.

ISBN 962·04·0226·X

CONTENTS

PREFACE

Shanghai is the largest industrial city as well as an important port in China. It is a municipality under the direct jurisdiction of the central government.

Situated on the coast of the East China Sea, it has a temperate climate with four distinct seasons. The municipality covers a total area of 6,192 square kilometers, of which the urban districts occupy 220. The total population is over 11 million, of which more than 6 million live in the urban area. The city proper is divided into 12 districts, while the suburbs are made up of 10 counties with more than 200 rural people's communes, which have developed a diversified economy of farming, forestry, animal husbandry, sideline production and fishery in addition to some industries.

The city has numerous rivers with the Huangpu as the largest, which flows through both suburban and urban Shanghai and joins the Changjiang (Yangtze) at the Mouth of Wusong.

Shanghai is a city with a glorious revolutionary tradition. The Communist Party of China was founded here in July 1921. The city was liberated in May 1949. Through the growth over the last 30 years and more, Shanghai has become a comprehensive industrial base almost complete with all branches of enterprises as well as a center of science, technology and culture.

Shanghai, though an industrial city with about 7,000 factories, has quite a number of scenic spots, historic sites and places of interest, which are attractions for tourists from all over the world.

This handbook, besides giving a general picture of the city, provides the reader with such information as where to find good accommodations, where to get a sampling of the famous cuisines and where best to do shopping, and so on.

It is hoped that this book will be of some help to the reader who is visiting or planning to visit the city.

KNOWING THE PLACE

Earliest Inhabitants

Each city has its own history of growth and development. Though Shanghai is not considered an old city by Chinese standards, archaeological finds suggest that Shanghai has a long history dating back five or six thousand years.

Archaeologists have located more than 20 sites in Shanghai and unearthed a large number of cultural artifacts dating back to some time between the Neolithic Age and the 3rd century B.C. These sites are found in places west of Gangshen and in the Gangshen area itself, which are in the western part of the municipality. From the site of Maqiao in the vicinity of Gangshen were excavated ancient shelters and tombs, stone tools, clay utensils and ornaments made of jade. These finds show that human beings began to settle here 4,500 years ago.

A Neolithic site with a history of 4,000 years was found in the Zhelin area in Fengxian County. Relics dating back 5,800-5,900 years were discovered at the Songze site in Qingpu County. It is possible that Songze was inhabited earlier than Maqiao and Zhelin. We may safely say that the earliest inhabitants in Shanghai were the people of Songze in Qingpu County.

Changes of the City of Shanghai

'Shen', 'Hu' and 'Shanghai'

As early as the Warring States period (475-221 B.C.), the western part of present-day Shanghai belonged to the State of Chu and was part of the domain of Huang Xie, a famous nobleman in Chinese history. His title was the King of Chun Shen, hence Shanghai is also called 'Chun Shen' or 'Shen' for short.

In the Jin Dynasty (A.D. 265-316) the residents along the Songjiang River (now known as the Suzhou Creek) and in the coastal area mainly lived on fishing. They used to set up a kind of bamboo tool named 'Hu' in the water for fishing. At high tide the 'Hu' was submerged underwater, but at low tide it would come above the water surface with fish caught inside it. Since the place where the river emptied into the sea was called 'Du' and it was where people employed the 'Hu', the area along the lower reaches of the Songjiang River was generally referred to as 'Hu Du'. That is how Shanghai came to be called 'Hu' for short.

The name 'Shanghai' appeared a little later. In the middle of the 13th century (during the Song Dynasty), ships from afar used to anchor in the Shanghai River, which was a branch of the Songjiang River. Cargoes were loaded and unloaded on the west bank of the river, where a town soon developed. The county of Shanghai was officially set up here in 1291 (in the Yuan Dynasty). The name 'Shanghai' derives from the Shanghai River, which submerged long ago. It is believed that the former river now lies in the Huangpu River, somewhere between the waterfront at Nanjing Road and the Shiliupu Wharf.

Shanghai in different ages

During the Xia Dynasty (21-16 c. B.C.)

the people of the Xia clan had already begun migrating to the south from Shandong, Shanxi, Gansu and Henan provinces and integrated with the Yue people, who lived in the area of Jiangsu and Zhejiang provinces and had an old civilization. According to one legend, the sixth emperor of the Xia Dynasty, Shao Kang, enfeoffed one of his sons in Huiji, who thereupon established the kingdom of Wuyu. The people of this kingdom opened up some land in present-day Jinshan County (within the municipal boundary of Shanghai) for cultivation.

The Xia Dynasty was later replaced by the Shang (16-11 c. B.C.). In the 11th century B.C. a Shang military expedition brought today's Anhui and Zhejiang provinces under its rule. Jiangsu, Zhejiang and Shanghai thus became dependencies offering tributes to the political regime in the central plains.

Before the founding of the Western Zhou Dynasty (11 c.-771 B.C.), a branch of the Zhou clan moved down to the east coast along the Changjiang (Yangtze River) and settled in the areas of today's Changzhou, Wuxi and Suzhou, where the kingdom of Gouwu was founded. Shanghai was then in the eastern border area of the kingdom.

During the Spring and Autumn period (770-476 B.C.), the area west of Gangshen in Shanghai, once covered by water, had already formed into a piece of land. At that time the people of Shanghai practised slash-and-burn farming and had already known the skill of smelting. By the time of the Warring States Shanghai belonged to the state of Chu, where a standard currency was in circulation.

During the Qin (211-207 B.C.) and Han (206 B.C. — A.D. 8) dynasties, the western part of present-day Shanghai belonged to the county of Lou, Huiji Prefecture. Coining, iron-smelting and salt-making were then the three major sources of income for the treasury. Shanghai, as one of the most important salt-producing areas, was already an important place.

During the Northern and Southern Dynasties (420-589) and the period of Sui (581-618) and early Tang (618-907), Shanghai was part of the Kunshan County, Wu Prefecture. Towards the middle of the Tang Dynasty a large seawall was built. As a result, the alluvial soil deposits accumulated more rapidly, and arable land increased day by day. Meanwhile, the population grew. In the year 751, the new county of Huating was set up in today's Songjiang area. Consisting of a large area, which included today's Hongkou district, Huating County faced the sea to the south, Xiasha to the east and Huating Sea to the northeast. The Songjiang River, with a width of 10 kilometers at its lower course, was the channel through which merchant ships of all kinds sailed in and out. On the western bank of the river and northwest of the Qingpu district (east of present-day Baihe and north of Chonggu) was established the town of Qinglong. With the continuous development of trade, Qinglong became a large commercial town on the southeast coast of the country.

By the Song Dynasty (60-1279), the greater part of present-day Shanghai had already emerged as a piece of land. At the same time, the upper reaches of the Songjiang had been silting up and the navigable course became narrower and narrower, so that big merchant ships could no longer pass through. As a consequence, the commercial center in Qinglong gradually moved to the region northeast of Huating. There, in that region lying in the present-day old town area, the customs department of 'Shibo Tiju Si' and the foreign trade market of 'Quehuo Chang' were established in 1074. As all incoming and outgoing ships passed through the Shanghai River and did their loading and unloading on its west bank, the region came to be called the township of Shanghai. It soon became a busy port of call and a center of trade with a big population. Large numbers of businessmen gathered here and foreign merchants also came to do business. The administrative and financial officials, who were originally in the town of Qinglong, moved over to Shanghai, which gradually replaced Qinglong as a trade center. Around 1265-1267, in the Southern Song Dynasty, Shanghai was officially established as a township, where troops were stationed, offices, schools, temples, restaurants, stores and living quarters were built. As a result, Shanghai became the largest township in Huating County.

In 1292 (the Yuan Dynasty), the town of Shanghai, together with four other towns in the northeast of Huating County, formed the county of Shanghai. This newly formed county, which covered today's urban Shanghai, as well as the counties of Shanghai, Qingpu, Nanjui and Chuansha, came under the jurisdiction of Songjiang

Prefecture. The former Songjian River was renamed the Wusong River.

In the 14th century, the Fanjiabang Canal was dredged and widened. It formed that part of today's Huangpu River from the Waibaidu Bridge downstream. Wide and deep, this canal-river played an important part in the economic development of Shanghai, making it a famous city in southeast China.

After the middle of the Ming Dynasty (1368-1644), areas on the southeast coast suffered greatly from piracy. To guard against the pirates, a city wall was built in 1553. The wall was located on what is today's Renmin Road and was preserved until 1912. The present old City God Temple was then the center of the county seat.

Early in the Qing Dynasty (1644-1911), marine transportation and trade became more developed. With the rise of European capitalism, foreigners frequented the coastal areas to seek markets, sell their surplus goods and trade opium. The Huangpu River swarmed with masts and sails; ships plied between ports along the Chinese coast and the southeast Asian countries. In 1685 the Qing government set up the customs service in Shanghai. By that time the city already had a population of 200,000.

After the Opium War, Britain forced the Qing government into signing the Treaty of Nanjing. In 1842, Shanghai was opened as one of the five trade ports (Canton, Amoy, Fuzhou, Ningbo, and Shanghai). Soon afterwards, the American and French also made the Qing government sign unequal treaties, turning Shanghai into their trade port. From then on, foreign powers leased concessions by pressure, seized the customs, stationed troops, set up jails and police stations and obtained consular jurisdiction. Taking advantage of the various privileges, they dumped their surplus goods, opened banks, firms and factories, ran the public utilities and smuggled opium on a large scale. They also took Shanghai as a base for penetrating into China's inland by way of the Changjiang. During this period, Shanghai gradually changed from an important town in southeast China into a city of semi-colonial and semi-feudal nature, with a lopsidedly developed industry and trade.

In 1948, Shanghai's population increased to 5,200,000. In the city, polarization was shocking. On one side, there were the high buildings of the rich, and on the other, the slums of the poor.

In May 1949, Shanghai was liberated and returned to the embrace of the Chinese people. Around 1960, in order to meet the needs of the development of production and the construction of the city, 10 counties (Shanghai, Jiading, Baoshan, Chuansha, Nanhui, Fengxian, Songjiang, Jinshan, Qingpu and Chongming) were incorporated into the municipality of Shanghai. The urban area of Shanghai consists of 12 districts — Xuhui, Jing'an, Changning, Luwan, Huangpu, Hongkou, Zhabei, Yangpu, Putuo, Nanshi, Minghang and Wusong. The total area of the municipality is 6,185 sq. km.

In the last thirty years and more,

Shanghai has developed into the largest comprehensive base in the country for industry, scientific research and foreign trade. In the future, it will certainly play an ever increasing role in the country's economy and develop into a prosperous and modernized city.

Streets of Shanghai — Old and New

Visitors who had been to Shanghai before 1949 may now find the names of some streets radically changed. The following is a list of such streets which had taken new names in the course of time.

Former Name	Name Now in Use
Avenue Road	Beijing Road (W)
Boulevard des Deux Republiques	Renmin Road
Boundary Road	Tianmu Road (E)
Rue Bourgeat	Changle Road
Bubbling Well Road	Nanjing Road (W)
The Bund	Zhongshan Road (E1)
Brenan Road	Changning Road
Rue Brenier de Montmorand	Madang Road
Broadway	Daming Road
Broadway East	Daming Road (E)
Canton Road	Guangdong Road
Route Cardinal Mercier	Maoming Road (S)
Carter Road	Shimen Road (2)
Columbia Road	Fanyu Road
Rue du Consulat	Jinling Road (E)
Route Conty	Jianguo Road (E)
Dalny Road	Dalian Road
Route R. Delastre	Taiyuan Road

Former Name	Name Now in Use
Route Doumer	Donghu Road
Route L. Dufour	Wulumuqi Road (S)
East Seward Road	Changzhi Road (E)
Edinburgh Road	Jiangsu Road
Avenue Edward VII	Yan'an Road (E)
Avenue Foch West Section	Yan'an Road (C)
Avenue Foch East Section	Jinling Road (W)
Foochow Road	Fuzhou Road
Route J. Frelupt	Jianguo Road (W)
Route Ghisi	Yueyang Road
Great Western Road	Yan'an Road (W)
Route Gustave de Boissenzon	Fuxing Road (W)
Avenue Haig	Huashan Road
Honan Road	Henan Road (C)
Jessfield Road	Wanhangdu Road
Avenue Joffre	Huaihai Road (C)
Kiukiang Road	Jiujiang Road
Rue Kraetzer	Jinling Road (C)
Route Lafayette	Fuxing Road (C)
Lincoln Avenue	Tianshan Road
Rue L. Lorton	Xiangyang Road (N)
Route A. Magy	Wulumuqi Road (C)
Rue Massenet	Sinan Road
Boulevard de Montigny	Xizang (Tibet) Road (S)
Moulmein Road	Maoming Road (N)
Nanking Route	Nanjing Road (E)
North Honan Road	Henan Road (N)
Peking Road	Beijing Road (E)
Route Pere Robert	Ruijin Road (2)
Avenue Petain	Hengshan Road
Route Pichon	Fenyang Road
Route Mgr. Prosper Paris	Tianping Road

Former Name	Name Now in Use
Quai de France	Zhongshan Road (E2)
Route Ratard	Julu Road
Robinson Road	Changshou Road
Avenue du Roi Albert	Shaanxi Road (S)
Route de Say-Zoong	Changshu Road
Seward Road	Changshi Road
Seymour Road	Shangxi Road (N)
Route H. de Sieyes	Yongjia Road
Singming Road	Tianmu Road (C)
Route des Soeurs	Ruijin Road (1)
Route Stanislas Chevalier	Jianguo Road (C)
Route Tenant de la Tour	Xiangyang Road (S)
Tifeng Road	Wulumuqi Road (N)
Ward Road	Changyang Road
Route J. Winling	Wanping Road
Yates Road	Shimen Road (1)
Yu Ya Ching Road	Xizang Road (C)
Zao Char Road	Fuxing Road (E)

Rivers and Lakes

Shanghai has many rivers and lakes forming a large network of waterways. Here we mainly introduce the Huangpu River, the Suzhou Creek and the Dianshan Lake.

Huangpu River

The Huangpu River rises from the Tai Lake. In its upper reaches at Mishidu, Songjiang County, it receives three main streams: Xietang from the Dianshan Lake, Maogang in Jiaxing County and Yuanxiejing near Pingwang. From the Dianshan Lake, one of its sources, the Huangpu River flows through six counties (Qingpu, Songjiang, Fengxian, Shanghai, Chuansha and Baoshan) and the city of Shanghai, and then joins the Changjiang at the Mouth of Wusong. The total length of the Huangpu River is approximately 110 km. It is about 83 km. in length from Mishidu to the Mouth of Wusong. The length of its lower reaches that go through the industrial area and the densely populated urban districts is somewhere around 39 km. The river is wide and deep and the water flow is slow. The Suzhou Creek is its biggest tributary.

Suzhou Creek

The Suzhou Creek was formerly called the Wusong River. Rising from the Tai Lake, it flows through Wujiang, Wuxian, Kunshan, Qingpu and Jiading counties and the city of Shanghai and runs into the Huangpu River at the Waibaidu Bridge. The Suzhou Creek is about 125 km. long and about 40-50 m. wide. The middle section varies in width with the narrowest point being 400 m. and the widest, 600-700 m.

The Suzhou Creek is the main waterway from Shanghai to the Tai Lake basin. Now, there are about 2 million people and 500-600 factories of different kinds along the banks of the creek.

Dianshan Lake

The Dianshan Lake, connected with the Huangpu River and the Suzhou Creek, is located between Qingpu County in Shanghai and Kunshan County in Jiangsu Province. The surface area of water is about 60 square kilometers and the average depth is two meters. It was once part of the ancient Tai Lake. There was a hill called the Dianshan Hill in the southeastern part of the lake, hence the name 'Dianshan Lake'.

The Dianpu Canal, rising from the lake and flowing east to the Huangpu River, is 46 km. long. It was dug in 1977.

The Dianshan Lake teems with crucian carp and bream and is an ideal ground for freshwater fish farming. Crabs from the lake are known as blue-shell crabs. Although they are not as large as those in the Yangcheng Lake, they are fleshy and extremely delicious.

There are quite a few places of interest around the lake, for example:
130-year-old Qushui Garden;
Site of ancient town Qinglong;
Mao Pagoda of the Tang Dynasty;
Longevity Pagoda of the Qing Dynasty;
Puji Bridge, the oldest arch stone bridge in Shanghai;
Fangsheng Bridge, the biggest arch stone bridge preserved intact;
Yingxiang Bridge;
Guan Wang Temple, built in 1640, commemorating the God of Chivalry, Guan Yu; and
Songze Archaeological Site.

The Dianshan Lake has been chosen as a priority tourist area. Along the shores of the lake will be built Chinese-styled pavilions and terraces. A mid-lake pavilion is under construction. While the eastern part of the lake will be allotted for swimming and rowing, shopping centers and a sanatorium will be built on the west shore.

Climate

With four distinct seasons, Shanghai has a short spring and autumn, while its summer and winter last longer. Its climate is generally temperate and humid. However, in winter Shanghai may experience a few severely cold days with a dry, cold north-west wind. In summer, a short spell of intense heat may attack Shanghai, though it usually enjoys many humid days with a warm southeast wind. The annual rainfall is moderate and equally distributed among the four seasons.

The four seasons are normally divided as follows:

Spring, from April 1st to June 4th (65 days)

Summer, from June 5th to September 22nd (110 days)

Autumn, from September 23rd to November 26th (65 days)

Winter, from November 27th to March 31st (125 days)

Spring

When spring comes to Shanghai, the cold northwest wind gets weaker. In April the wind is mostly southeasterly and the average temperature rises above 10°C. The amount of rainfall increases considerably. Very often the weather alternates between several days of fine weather and several days of rain. Sometimes there may also be consecutive days of rain or fine weather. Due to the interchange of cold and hot air masses, Shanghai is often attacked by sudden spells of cold and hot weather in spring. The temperature fluctuates so drastically that it

may differ by 10°C within two days. No
wonder the saying goes, 'When you travel
in spring, take the clothing for three seasons
with you.'

Summer

When summer comes, the plum ripens,
marking the beginning of 'plum rain'. * The
'plum rain' season normally lasts about 20
days from mid June to early July. However,
in some years there may be no such 'plum
rain' season and the rainy weather lasts for
only a few days. In other years the 'plum rain'
season can last as long as 40 days. Generally,
at the beginning of the 'plum rain' season the
temperature rises noticeably, but the average
never exceeds 22°C. At this time, the
relative humidity is usually above 85%, and
very often the weather changes abruptly
from sunshine to rain or vice versa. In the
middle of the season the temperature is
between 23°C and 25°C with the maximum
generally below 30°C. The relative humidity
is usually above 95%. The wind is mild and
there may be consecutive days of rain. Near
the end of the season the temperature
averages 26° to 27°C with the highest above
30°C. However, extremely hot days with the
temperature above 35°C are rare. Thunder
storms are common.

After mid July, Shanghai experiences
a mid summer with long periods of fine
but hot weather. Every year it has about
15 to 20 dog days with the temperature

* (plum rain, *mei yu*, is a Chinese literary jargon
  referring to the raining in the areas around
  the Changjiang and River Huai where plum
  blossoms bloom luxuriantly in summer)

hovering between 35°C and 38°C. It seldom exceeds 38°C. However, after several days of a hot southwest wind, there will be a stretch of sweltering hot weather, which brings along intense heat.

Autumn

September brings early autumn to Shanghai, when there are about 10 days of autumn rain, which is usually heavy, often in showers, accompanied by thunderstorms and strong winds. Occasionally there is a year in which the rainy period lasts as long as 15-20 days, a year of what we call 'long autumn rain'. In some years the autumn rainy period never appears, and the summer heat continues, which is what we call 'autumn tiger' weather. However, the hot autumn period does not last long. It is often hot at noon but cool in the morning and evening.

From late September to late October, Shanghai is in a fresh 'new autumn' period, which is characterized by little rain, an agreeable climate and a clear sky. As Tao Yuaming, a famous poet of the Eastern Jin Dynasty, put it, 'The four seasons are all good, but the best is the new autumn period.'

Winter

Winter comes to Shanghai in December and is marked by the prevalence of a northwest seasonal wind from Inner Mongolia and periods of cold, dry and clear weather. There are about 10 days when the temperature averages below 0°C. Occasionally Shanghai is hit by a 'cold wave' coming down from the north.

Generally, snowfall in Shanghai begins as early as late December and ends as late as mid March. There is an average of 7.2 days of snow a year.

TEMPERATURE BY MONTH (in °C)
(Source: Shanghai Municipal Weather Bureau)

Month	Monthly Average	Average Maximum	Average Minimum
January	3.3	7.8	0.0
February	4.3	8.7	1.0
March	8.3	13.1	4.5
April	13.8	19.1	19.8
May	18.9	24.3	14.9
June	23.2	28.1	19.7
July	27.4	32.3	24.0
August	27.4	32.5	24.0
September	23.2	28.2	19.8
October	17.7	23.2	13.7
November	11.7	17.0	7.7
December	5.9	10.9	2.1

Transport

Transport in the city proper of Shanghai is convenient. Travelers may go by buses, trolley-buses and taxis (for detailed information on bus routes, please see the map attached). From Shanghai, travelers can go by train to all the other major Chinese cities. Every day, there are 37 passenger trains pulling in and out of the Shanghai Station.

Shanghai is connected with major ports round the world by sea routes. Since 1980, a new sea route from Shanghai to Xianggang (Hongkong) has been put into operation. A relatively modern domestic passenger terminal

— Shiliupu Wharf — has been inaugurated recently.

Air Transport

Domestic and international lines are operated by the Civil Aviation Administration of China (CAAC). One of the major routes is the Beijing-Shanghai-Nagasaki-Osaka-Tokyo line.

The CAAC booking office is located at 789 Yan'an Road (C), tel. 532255. For flight information, call 537664 at the airport.

Shanghai Friendship Taxi/Bus Company

The Company operates with majestic and luxurious 'Red Flag' limousines, comfortable 'Shanghai' sedans, mini-buses for passengers or cargo and tourist buses. It offers prompt service round-the-clock. Its taxis are available at the airport, the railway station and the major hotels. The tourist may call them at any time or arrange for them in advance.

The Firsts and Superlatives of Shanghai

The earliest Shanghailanders were those who settled in the Songze area, Qingpu County, 5,800 to 5,900 years ago.

The highest point of elevation in Shanghai is the peak of the Tianma Mountain in Songjiang County, 97.9 meters above sea level.

The lowest area in Shanghai is the Dianmao area in the western part of

Shanghai, most of which is only two or three meters above sea level.

The highest temperature recorded in Shanghai was 40.2°C on July 12, 1934.

The lowest temperature recorded in Shanghai was −12.1°C on January 19, 1893.

The largest amount of annual rainfall in Shanghai was 1,602 mm in 1931.

The smallest amount of annual rainfall in Shanghai was 709.2 m in 1892.

The heaviest snowfall in Shanghai was in the period from the end of 1968 to the beginning of 1969, with altogether 16 days of snow.

The first broadcasting station in Shanghai was set up in 1923.

The first mechanized plant in Shanghai was the Jiangnan Manufactory, set up in 1865.

The highest structure in Shanghai is the Shanghai Television Tower, 210 meters in height.

The highest building in Shanghai is the Shanghai Hotel, over 90 meters in height (higher than the 83.7 -meter-high Park Hotel).

The first university run by the Chinese in Shanghai was the Nanyang Public College (later turned into the Jiaotong University), founded in 1896 (the 22nd year of the regin of Emperor Guang Xu in the Qing Dynasty).

The first public library in Shanghai was

the Shanghai Library, set up in 1849 (the 29th year of the reign of Emperor Dao Guang of the Qing Dynasty).

The first Shanghai newspaper in Chinese was the *New Shanghai Daily*, published in December, 1861 (the 11th year of the reign of Emperor Xian Feng of the Qing Dynasty).

The first movie house in Shanghai was the Hongkou Theater, built in 1908 (the 34th year of the reign of Emperor Guang Xu of the Qing Dynasty).

The largest movie house in Shanghai is Da Guang Ming (the former Grand Theater), with a seating capacity of 1,906.

The biggest recreation center in Shanghai is the present Shanghai Municipal Youth Palace, the former Great World.

The biggest park in Shanghai is the Shanghai Zoo covering a total area of 70 hectares.

The largest department store in Shanghai is the No. 1 Department Store, with over 1,000 counters and a total floor space of some 18,000 square meters.

The biggest market in Shanghai dealing in small articles is the Yu Garden Bazaar with 122 special stores handling some 16,000 kinds of commodities.

The biggest silk store in Shanghai is the Shanghai Silk Fabric Store.

The first store in Shanghai dealing in special styles of men's and women's leather shoes is the Zhonghua Leather Shoe Store, set up in 1917.

The largest book store in Shanghai is the Xinhua Book Store on Nanjing Road (E).

The longest street in Shanghai proper is Zhongshan Ring Road totalling 29,050 meters in length.

The broadest street in the city proper is the People's Avenue, about 40 meters wide.

The busiest street in Shanghai is Nanjing Road. In this five-kilometer-long street, there are over 330 stores.

The most beautiful boulevard in Shanghai is Zhaojiabang Road, also called Green Island Street.

ACCOMMODATION

Jinjiang Hotel
59 Maoming Rd., tel. 534242

The Jinjiang Hotel stands on Maoming Rd., north of Huaihai Rd. in the center of the city. There are 4 buildings and a club. The north building was formerly the Cathay Mansions, built in 1929. It is 65 meters in height. The central building (the former Grosvenor House), put up in 1935, has 18 stories and is 78 meters high. The west building consists of six blocks of three-storied castle-like structures, which were accessories to the former Grosvenor House. It was built in 1934 and is 18 meters high. The south building was put up in 1965 and has 5 stories. It is 21.5 meters in height. There are altogether 706 rooms with 1,400 beds. Among them the deluxe suites are used to receive state guests and also to accommodate foreign tourists and businessmen.

Each building has its own dining hall, which serves Sichuan and Guangzhou (Cantonese) dishes as well as Yangzhou and Sichuan pastries and refreshments. Fujian, Hunan and Shanghai specialities are also available in addition to French, European and American dishes and pastries. Banquets and dinner parties can be ordered in advance.

There is a shopping mall in the hotel. Along one side of the mall are the Front Desk, a PTT office, a foodstuff shop, a gift shop, a barber shop, a foreign languages book store, a snack bar and a cafe, where visitors can shop and get different kinds of services.

There is a small auditorium built in 1959 inside the hotel compound. It can be used as a meeting hall or as a theater.

The Jinjiang Club is opposite to the hotel. It has a grand ballroom, a billiard room, a bowling alley, an electric games room and a tennis court surrounded by a large beautiful garden. The club has a snack bar and a banquet hall serving Chinese and western foods, but mainly French cuisine.

The hotel is 6 kilometers from the railway station, 14 kilometers from the airport.

Peace Hotel
20 Nanjing Rd. (E)., tel. 211244

The Peace Hotel stands on Nanjing Road by the Huangpu River. It has one building on each side of the road. The building on the north side is the former Cathay Hotel. The construction was started in 1926 and completed in 1929. It is a 77-meter-high building with 11 stories and a basement. It is the first tall building ever put up on the waterfront. The building on the south side was the former Palace Hotel. It is a five-storied structure built in 1906. The hotel has altogether 338 rooms with 663 beds. Among them 9 suites are furnished in the styles of 9 different countries, namely, China, Japan, the United States, Britain, Germany, India, Italy, Spain and France.

The hotel has a spacious dining hall and offers catering services for banquets and dinner parties besides regular meals. The Peace Dining Hall is a structure of graceful proportions and well-matched colors. The Dragon-Phoenix Dining Hall with dragon-phoenix bas-relief on the ceiling represents the traditional style of the country. Sitting in the Dragon-Phoenix Hall, one can watch the ships sailing on the river and enjoy the beautiful scenery on its banks. The Peace Hotel offers both Chinese and western foods. The Chinese food includes Shanghai, Guangzhou and Sichuan cuisines. But it best serves Shanghai food and excels in French food. Good coffee is served in the cafe there.

The hotel has other facilities, such as a post office, a foreign exchange counter, a retail shop, a barber shop (with massage service), a taxi service desk, a foreign languages bookstore and a billiard room.

The hotel is 18 kilometers from the airport, 2.5 kilometers from the railway station.

Shanghai Mansions
20 Suzhou Rd. (N), tel. 246260

The hotel used to be called the Broadway Mansions. Its construction was started in 1930 and completed in 1934. It was renamed the Shanghai Mansions in 1951. The building is 78.3 meters high with twenty-two stories above ground.

The hotel is located at the junction of the Huangpu River and the Suzhou Creek. The top of the Mansions is a place that affords an excellent view of the city. The main building is used to accommodate foreign guests, overseas Chinese and visitors from Xianggang (Hongkong), Aomen (Macao) and Taiwan. It has 249 rooms with 498 beds. The subordinate building (namely the Pujiang Hotel) is for domestic guests. With 121 rooms, it can lodge 973 people.

The hotel mainly provides Yangzhou and

French dishes and snacks. The dining room caters for large parties. The hotel has a barber shop (with massage service available), a coffee room, a post office, a foreign exchange desk, a taxi service desk, a billiard table and an electric games room.

The hotel is 18 kilometers from the airport, 3 kilometers from the railway station.

Park Hotel
(Guoji Fandian)
170 Nanjing Rd. (W), tel. 225225

The Park Hotel was constructed by the former Sihang Savings Association. It was designed by a Hungarian architect and built by a Chinese contractor. The construction started in 1932 and the hotel was opened in December 1934. At that time, it was the

One of the 116 rooms in the Park Hotel

highest building in the Far East. It has 24 stories and contains 116 rooms and 7 dining rooms, which can serve more than two thousand people at one sitting.

After 1949, the hotel opened its doors to the general public. At present, the Shunfeng Hall in the basement supplies coffee and cakes. A shop on the first floor sells popular pastries and refreshments. The Fengze Chamber on the second floor serves genuine Beijing dishes. The restaurant on the third floor offers French cuisine. The Peacock Hall on the fourteenth floor provides Beijing dishes and catering services for parties. Restaurants on the fifteenth, eighteenth and nineteenth floors are always ready to accept reservations for dinner parties. The nineteenth floor has a commanding view of Shanghai. One may even take in the Mouth of Wusong in the distance on a clear day.

The hotel is 15 kilometers from the airport, 2 kilometers from the railway station.

Hengshan Guest House
534 Hengshan Rd., tel. 377050

The Hengshan Guest House, constructed in 1936, was called the Piccardilly Mansions. It is a fifteen-storied building, 65 meters high. In 1960, it was remodelled into a guest house. Since the Hengshen Guest House is located in the southwest of Shanghai, the environment is peaceful and secluded. It has 87 rooms (including singles, suites and deluxe suites) with 390 beds. Its dining hall and banquet hall were built in 1979. They can be used to hold large banquets and cocktail parties. The hotel provides Chinese and western dishes and refreshments of fine

quality. The distinguished feature of the
food served there is Sichuan cuisine.
Genuine French dishes are also offered in
the hotel.

The Hengshan has a bar, a coffee room, a
foreign exchange counter, a post office, a
bookstore, a department store, a barber
shop, a taxi service counter, etc. It is 12
kilometers from the airport, 9 kilometers
from the railway station.

Overseas Chinese Hotel
(Huaqiao Fandian)
104 Nanjing Rd. (W), tel. 226226

The predecessor of the Overseas Chinese
Hotel was the Hua-An-He-Qun Life
Insurance Company. In 1938 it was turned
into the Golden Gate Hotel. In 1958 it was
renamed the Overseas Chinese Hotel.

The hotel is located at the downtown
section of Nanjing Road to the east of the
Park Hotel. It faces the People's Park with
beautiful environment and good transport
facilities. The nine-storied building, 38.7
meters in height, was constructed in 1924.
The hotel is marked by tall marble columns,
beams and walls on the front. On top of the
hotel roof there is a 9-meter-high clock
tower with a gilded dome. On the second
floor there is a shop, a coffee room, a
foreign exchange counter, a post office, a
taxi service desk, an electric games room, the
hotel's reception desk and the service desk
of the China Travel Service. The guest rooms
are on the floors from the third up to the
seventh. There are 177 beds in 95 rooms,
among which five are suites. There are
banquet halls of different styles on the

eighth and ninth floors and at the eastern end of the first floor. The Dragon-Phoenix Hall and the Pine-Crane Hall, two of the seven dining halls on the ninth floor, are elegantly furnished with a traditional Chinese touch.

The hotel supplies Fujian, Guangzhou and Chaozhou dishes, as well as Chinese and western pastries. Among the Chaozhou and Fujian dishes served are 'Fo Tiao Qiang' (sea food and poultry in casserole), pork chop marinated in wine, duck flavored with brewer's grain, stewed shark's fin, chicken in satay paste, beef brochette and fried fish fillet.

Jing'an Guest House
370 Huashan Rd., tel. 563050

The Jing'an Guest House was formerly the Haig Apartment House. It was built by Haig, a German, in 1925. After 1949 it was converted into an office building. In order to meet the needs of the fast developing tourist industry, it was reconstructed into a hotel in 1977 and named after the former well-known Jing'an Temple nearby.

The guest house, 43 meters high, has nine stories in its original Spanish architectural style. It has 104 rooms with 208 beds, of which one is a deluxe suite. The dining hall and the banquet hall are on the eighth floor and the ninth floor respectively. At the same time, the guest house supplies Yangzhou and French dishes. It has a retail shop, a book and painting shop, a post office, a coffee room, a barber shop (with massage service), and an electric games room.

The guest house is 13 kilometers from the

airport and 7 kilometers from the railway station.

Dahua Guest House
914 Yanan Rd. (W), tel. 523079

Formerly known as the Dahua Apartment House, the hotel is a 38.5-meter-high, ten-storied building built between 1934 and 1937. As its design and building materials are similar to those of the Park Hotel, it is also called 'The little Park Hotel'. It has 90 rooms with 180 beds, of which 2 are deluxe suites.

A four-storied hotel restaurant consisting of dining rooms and banquet halls has been put up recently on the east side of the hotel building. The restaurant offers Beijing and French foods. All-duck, all-fish, and all-dimsum dinners as well as Japanese food can be ordered in advance.

The hotel has a shop, a cafe, a bar, a barber shop (with massage service), a post office and a bank.

The hotel is 10 km. from the airport and 7 km. from the railway station.

CUISINES

To meet the various demands of visitors from all parts of the country and of the world, restaurants serving different regional cuisines and western food have been set up. Sixteen kinds of regional cooking, such as Beijing, Shanghai and Guangzhou foods, are available in Shanghai. English, French, German, Italian and Russian cuisines are also available.

Famous Restaurants

Shanghai Old Town Restaurant
Lao Fandian
242 Fuyou Road, tel. 282782

This is a restaurant noted for its local Shanghai flavor. Formerly called 'Rongshunguan' set up during the reign of Emperor Tong Zhi of the Qing Dynasty, it has a history of more than a hundred years. As time went by, people simply called it the 'Old Restaurant' for short. The cookery of the restaurant is well-known for its cooking with generous amounts of oil and its stewing with soy sauce. Dishes worth mentioning are 'sauté pork chop', 'boiled deep-fried pork braised in soy sauce with clover', 'braised black carp chin and tail', 'assorted three-flavor dish' and 'eight-treasure duck'.

Great Fortune Restaurant
Dahongyun Jiulou
556 Fuzhou Road, tel. 223176

Opened in 1931 and moved to Fuzhou Road in 1935, it covers a floor space of 2,500 square meters, large enough for holding 100 tables. Its famous dishes are 'stir-fried minced crab', 'coined egg white and white mushroom sweet soup', 'chicken, ham, mushroom and water mallow soup' and 'fried potato with egg in bird's nest shape'.

People's Restaurant
Renmin Fandian
226 Nanjing Road (W), tel. 533475

It is formerly known as the Wuweizhai Restaurant North Branch, and is famous for its fine cookery. The famous dishes are 'five-flavor chicken drumstick', 'walnut and chicken roll' and 'fried minced crab'.

Yanyunlou Restaurant
Yanyun Lou
755 Nanjing Road (E), tel. 223293

The restaurant is noted for its Beijing food. Famous dishes include 'Beijing duck', 'stewed bear's paw', 'assorted vegetables',

Mandarin fish with pine nuts — a famous dish

'fish in pepper and vinegar sauce' and 'double-flavor fruit toffee'. The third floor is reserved for foreign guests.

Dongfeng Hotel
Dongfeng Fandian
3 Zhongshan Road (1), tel. 218060

The restaurant in this hotel serves famous dishes, such as 'prawn in brown sauce', 'Dongfeng chicken drumstick' and 'mandarin fish with three kinds of garniture'. It is one of the restaurant centers for training chefs in Shanghai. It caters for wedding banquets and serves Suzhou-style dishes.

Yangzhou Restaurant
Yangzhou Fandian
457 Nanjing Road (E), tel. 222779

It was formerly called Moyoucai's Kitchen, which catered exclusively for parties of industrialists and businessmen. It has such special dishes as 'sea cucumber in a butterfly pattern', 'minced crab with sliced dried beancurd', 'fried quail eggs' and 'preserved pork'.

Chengdu Restaurant
Chengdu Fandian
795 Huaihai Road (C), tel. 376412

There are four dining halls in this restaurant, which serves Sichuan food. 'Beggar chicken', 'crisp duck', 'braised sliced beef', 'braised crucian carp', etc. are its famous dishes. Apart from providing such as accepting orders through telephone, the restaurant caters for wedding banquets, delivers dishes to customers' homes and sends chefs over to prepare the dishes.

Sichuan Restaurant
Sichuan Fandian
457 Nanjing Road (E), tel. 222246

Set up in 1951 and moved to Nanjing Road (E) in 1957, it is a big restaurant serving Sichuan dishes. Its famous dishes are 'Guifei chicken', 'shrimp in two flavors', 'Nanjiang beancurd', 'sliced meat', 'shark's fin with egg white' and 'beef with shrimp'.

Meilongzhen Restaurant
Meilongzhen Jiujia
No. 22, Lane 1081, Nanjing Road (W), tel. 535353

Set up in 1938, the restaurant was orignally situated on Weihaiwei Road. Later it was moved to the present address. It is known for its Yangzhou and Sichuan dishes. In recent years, it has added some two hundred traditional dishes to its menu. Its famous dishes include 'stewed prawn', 'Longfeng meat' and 'crisp chicken'.

Xinya Guangzhou Restaurant
Xinya Yuecaiguan
719 Nanjing Road (E), tel. 224393

The Xinya Restaurant, set up in 1926, is located on the most bustling street of Shanghai. It has a seating capacity of 690 on three floors. On the first floor, Guangzhou dimsum and pastries are served. On the second floor there are three chambers and five separate rooms. On the third floor are the Baiyun Hall and the Yuexiu Hall serving foreign customers and overseas Chinese. On this floor there are more than twenty separate rooms. The restaurant is well-known for its 'sweet and sour pork', 'smoked pomfret', 'stir-fried egg white',

The famous 'Beijing roast duck' is usually sliced in front of guests – the Yanyunlou chefs are masters of this feat 'chicken with ham', 'fried custard' and 'crisp skin roast piglet'.

Luyangcun Restaurant
Luyangcun Jiujia
763 Nanjing Road (W), tel. 537221

This restaurant offers such famous Sichuan dishes as 'quick-fried rice', 'braised prawn', 'sliced black carp in pepper sauce', 'beef stewed with orange peel' as well as 'honeyed ham'. It also serves famous Yangzhou pastries, such as 'shredded turnip and ham savarin', 'emerald green dumplings filled with meat' and 'pancake with bamboo shoot and meat filling'. These can be either taken our or served in the restaurant. The three-storied restaurant with a four-bay facade and a base-ment has a seating capacity of 370. It serves banquets and snacks on all floors.

Xinghualou Restaurant
Xinghua Lou
343 Fuzhou Road, tel. 282747

It is a Guangzhou restaurant with a history of more than 120 years. The restaurant is housed in a four-storied building, large enough for holding 120 tables. It serves Guangzhou food, cured meat, moon cake, dimsum and pastry, and specializes in preparing banquets with snake dishes of Guangzhou taste.

Meixin Restaurant
Meixin Jiujia
314 Shaanxi Road (S), tel. 373991

It is a Guangzhou restaurant, set up in the 1920s. The famous dishes are 'saute sliced beef in oyster sauce', 'Qilin mandarin fish', 'braised abalone in crabapple pattern', 'shark's fin in plum pattern' and 'soup in a carved white gourd'.

Yueyanglou Restaurant
Yueyang Lou Yinshidian
28 Xizang Road (S), tel. 282670

It is a restaurant which serves Hunan cuisine. Famous dishes are 'Dong' an chicken', 'simmered chicken wing and foot and gizzard in soy sauce' and 'assorted dish of tripe in brown and white sauce'.

Muslim Restaurant
Qingzhen Fandian
710 Fuzhou Road, tel. 224876

It is the largest Muslim restaurant in Shanghai. Dishes like 'rinsed sliced mutton', (Mongolian hot pot) 'barbecued lamb', 'oiled chicken', 'duck in white sauce' and 'beef in soy sauce' are its specialties. The restaurant also prepares 'stewed mutton served with sauce' and 'mutton with rice'. It is the favorite restaurant of visitors from Muslim countries.

Gongdelin Vegetarian Restaurant
Gongdelin Sucaiguan
43 Huanghe Road, tel. 531313

This restaurant, established in 1922, has now a history of sixty years. The Gongdelin dishes, prepared with vegetables in a unique style, look and taste like fish and meat. Popular dishes are 'sliced fish in the shape of mandarin duck', 'crucian carp with bamboo shoot', 'sweet and sour croaker' and 'eight-treasure stuffed chicken'.

Jade Buddha Temple Vegetarian Restaurant
Yufosi Suzhai
170 Anyuan Road, tel. 535745

This restaurant is located inside the Jade Buddha Temple. It serves such special vegetarian dishes as 'fingered-citron-shaped bamboo shoot cooked in brewer's grain', 'silvery sliced mushroom', 'stuffed cubed beancurd' and 'emerald green ball'.

Deda Western Food Restaurant
Deda Xicaishe
359 Sichuan Road (C), tel. 213810

Set up in 1897, with a history of more than 80 years, it specializes in preparing German food in addition to selling European pastries, cream cake and coffee. In winter, it also serves Japanese-style hot pot — *Sukiyaki.*

The Red House
Hong Fangzi
37 Shaanxi Road (S), tel. 565748

The Red House is well-known for its French food. Its onion soup, soufflé grand marnier and other dishes are the delights to be enjoyed in China.

Introducing the Regional Cuisines

Shanghai Food

Using local produce, Shanghai cuisine is characterized by its ample use of gravy, oil and brown sauce. The original flavors of the ingredients are preserved. Its famous dishes are 'braised catfish in soy sauce', cooked over a moderate flame and served with thick gravy, which is tender and savory; 'meat cooked with brewer's grain in a jar'; and 'stir-fried fresh clover', which looks green and pleases one's palate.

Suzhou Food

Suzhou cuisine, started in Suzhou in the Ming Dynasty, has been developed from home cooking. The dishes are tender with a slight sweet flavor. Famous dishes are 'oiled duck', 'stewed meat with fermented beancurd flavor', 'steamed and braised chicken with chestnut' and 'shrimp in white sauce', etc.

Wuxi Food

It has originated from boat cooking on the Tai Lake, and is noted for its preparation of aquatic products. The black carp, for instance, can be prepared into 20 different dishes by using different parts of the fish. 'Black carp belly', 'braised black carp chin and tail', 'stir-fried minced crab' and 'stewed crucian carp with egg' are the famous dishes.

Beijing Food

Beijing cuisine provides a great variety of dishes that have won a fine reputation in the catering trade. It is said that Beijing cuisine was developed out of the imperial kitchen and the noble families. The Beijing cuisine introduced to Shanghai still maintains its original style and taste. The food is crispy, tender, fragrant and delicious. The famous dishes include 'quick-fried fish fillet flavored with brewer's grain', 'fried gizzard and tripe', and 'roast Beijing duck'. The Beijing duck with crispy skin and tender meat is famous throughout the world.

Yangzhou Food

Yangzhou food, palatable and tasty, is a general term for Zhenjiang and Yangzhou dishes. One of its distinctive traits is that the ingredients are finely sliced before the cooking process. As for the cookery, it stresses stewing and hard-boiling. It has a special way of preparing soup and broth. 'Meatball with minced crab', 'boiled shredded dried beancurd' and 'crucian carp stuffed with pork' are among the famous dishes.

Sichuan Food

The cuisine, represented by Chengdu cookery, is classified into meals and snacks. Vegetables are the main ingredients. It emphasizes seasoning and careful preparation of the seven tastes (sour, hot, piquant, bitter, sweet, fragrant, and salty) and eight flavors (dry braising, hot and pungent, stir-frying in sauce, sour and spicy, hot and spicy, quaint flavor, peppery and piquant and flavoring with cayenne oil). Each way of preparation has its own characteristic and taste, and each dish its own style. Sichuan cuisine in Shanghai, in the course of time, has been gradually modified to cater to the palate of the Shanghailander by reducing the spicy taste while preserving its special features and traditional ways of preparation. The famous dishes are 'Guifei chicken', 'diced chicken with pepper and soy sauce', 'duck smoked with black tea and camphor-wood', 'shredded pork with hot and pungent flavor', 'stewed crucian carp in sauce' and 'spiced beancurd'.

Guangzhou Food

So great is the influence of Guangzhou food in Shanghai that a 'Shanghai-style Guangzhou food' is developed with a fame of its own.

Guangzhou dishes stress freshness, tenderness and tastefullness. 'Plain stir-fried shrimp', 'beef with oyster sauce', 'sweet and sour pork', 'fried sliced chicken with egg white', 'stewed pomfret with scallion and oil' as well as 'roasted piglet' are the favorites of every gourmet.

Hunan Food

Hunan food, with a long history, is meticulously cooked and strong in local flavor. It is one of the eight major kinds of cuisines in China. Most of the dishes are sour and spicy. The famous dishes in Shanghai are 'Dong'an chicken', 'golden coin fish', 'simmered boned chicken wing, foot and gizzard in soy sauce', 'tenderloin with egg white' and 'hot-sour diced fish'.

Muslim food

Shanghai has two schools of muslim restaurants — the southern and the northern. The restaurants of the northern school use mutton and beef as the main culinary materials. The mutton is prepared by instant rinsing, roasting, saucing and quick-frying. Among the famous dishes are 'stir-fried tenderloin in soy sauce', 'instant-rinsed tripe', 'deep-fried sheep tail' and 'Ta-Si-Mi', which is a dish of sliced mutton mixed with sweet soy sauce and starch, and then deep-fried and served in thick sauce. Restaurants of the southern school have made a special study of chicken and duck. 'Pressed salted duck', 'oiled chicken' and 'marinated duck' are just some of their specialties.

Vegetarian food

Vegetarian food was originally served in Buddhist temples. At first, there were only local vegetarian dishes in Shanghai; later on, Yangzhou vegetarian dishes were introduced. The local vegetarian dishes are oily and substantial, but lacking in variety. The Yangzhou ones created by Yangzhou chefs are cooked in the same way as meat and fish. They are rich in variety and are named after meat and fish. These dishes with bean products and vegetables as ingredients are prepared to look like real chicken, duck, fish and meat. The famous dishes are 'stir-fried bamboo-shoot and mushroom', 'vegetarian ham' and 'fried vegetarian prawn'.

Some Popular Snacks of Shanghai

Nanxiang steamed dumpling

Nanxiang is one of the main towns on the outskirts of Shanghai. The steamed dumpling named after it is small and inviting, with translucent and chewy unleavened dough filled with choice ingredients, and holds much thick gravy. It tastes the best when eaten together with vinegar and shredded ginger.

Pigeon egg dumpling

'Pigeon egg dumpling' is served only at the Cassia Flower Chamber opposite to the Nine-Turn Bridge in the Old City. The snack shop is named after the cassia tree in front of it. The dumpling in the shape of a pigeon egg weighs 5 grams each. White glutinous rice of fine quality is made into the dough wrapper, which is filled with cassia flower syrup and peppermint. Each dumpling is kneaded into the shape of a pigeon egg and boiled in water. After it is taken out and left to cool, it is sprinkled with ground roasted sesame seeds. It is then placed on a broad reed leaf, ready to be sold.

Pigeon egg dumpling is glutinous, tender and smooth. It is served cool but not hard, soft but not sticky. Take a bite and you will enjoy the savor of the sweet and fragrant syrup.

Fried chicken bun

The bun is a very popular snack in Shanghai and is served all the year round. Different from other fried buns, it is filled with choice chicken meat. White wheat flour is used for making the leavened dough. The filling is made of cooked diced chicken, minced pork, jellied pig's skin and sesame oil. The bun is small, four buns weighing 50 grams. Every bun has about 15 pleats made by kneading and its top is dotted with sesame seeds or chopped scallions. After having been fried in oil the bun turns crispy and golden brown at the bottom with the upper half soft and saturated with oil. It has a large filling and plenty of gravy. It is best served right from the frying pan.

'Three shrimps' noodles

The 'three shrimps' are shrimp meat, shrimp brain and shrimp roe. Meat and brain are shelled from freshwater shrimps and stir-fried. To these, shrimp roe, soy sauce and other seasoning are added before they are fried over a high flame. To serve, the garniture is spooned over the noodles.

Xiekehuang cookie
(Crisp Savarin shaped as Crab Shell)

Round and yellow like the shell of a cooked crab, it tastes savory and rich with a flaky crust. The pastry of the cookie is made of raised dough kneaded with shortening into a flat round shape and coated with sesame seeds on the surface. It is then baked on a stove. Its stuffing is of two varieties, salty and sweet. The salty ones are flavored with pork, minced crab, shrimp, or scallion and fat, whereas the sweet ones are flavored with castor sugar, sugared rose petals, red bean puree or date mash. Ordinarily those with scallion and fat or castor sugar are sold in the market.

The cookies are preferably served hot to customers. They should be eaten with care so that the diners will not lose the delicious crisp flakes.

Crisp meat cookie

The cookie can either be baked or deep fried. It is golden brown, rich, flaky and crispy.

Eyebrow-shaped shortcake

The layers of this shortcake are like eyebrows with a flaky and crispy crust. There are two varieties, sweet and salty. The sweet cones have red bean puree, nuts and melon seed kernels as fillings, while the salty ones use pork and shrimp. The eyebrow shortcake elaborately prepared by the Lubolang Restaurant in the Yu Garden Bazaar is filled with finely shredded pork, bamboo shoot and champignon and is excellent in color, flavor and taste. It melts in one's mouth and is delicious beyond description.

Vegetarian moon cake by Gongdelin Restaurant

The vegetarian moon cake baked in the restaurant is a unique pastry. Ever since 1925, the restaurant has been producing moon cakes on the occasion of the Chinese Mid-Autumn Festival. The cake has a large filling, seasoned with sesame oil and sugar.

Shortpie of Gaoqiao Bakery

As one of the four noted pastries of the Gaoqiao Bakery, shortpie is no less famous than the other three, namely shortbread, crisp cookie and flaky shortcake. The cake is prepared with white flour, lard, castor sugar, red bean and cassia flowers as ingredients. Its crispy multi-layers and finely mashed bean filling provide a rich and delicate taste.

Egg 'shaqima' (Candied fritter)

There are two different interpretations of the name. People in the north suggest that it is a Manchurian name. However, according to people in the south, the name describes the process of making the snack.

Egg 'shaqima' is a popular snack of Guangdong style, with fine wheat flour, egg, peanut oil, maltose and granulated sugar as ingredients. No water is used in mixing the batter except egg, peanut oil, maltose and flour. The dough is then kneaded, sliced, deep fried, dipped in molasses and shaped into blocks. The product is yellow and has a golden lustre and a uniform block shape. It tastes sweet, soft and refreshing.

Suzhou crisp candy bar

The candy bar is also called 'crisp cake'. It is made of ingredients such as shelled pine nuts from the northeast, granulated sugar, glucose and so on. It is light yellow, with a glittering tint and looks pretty when wrapped in cellophane.

Crisp candy bar was first produced in Suzhou and later brought to Shanghai by the Suzhou Caizhizhai, which has been a famous confectionery chain for 200 years.

Western Pastry

Western pasrty in Shanghai is featured by cream cakes of Russian, French, German, Italian, English and American styles.

SIGHTSEEING

Scenic Spots and Places of Interest

Yu Garden

The Yu Garden is located in the Old Chinese City just beside the City God Temple. In front of the main entrance is a pool with a bridge of nine turnings leading to a pavilion. The garden was built around 1559-1579 in the Ming Dynasty by Pan Yunduan for his father Pan En, Minister of Justice, to enjoy a leisure life during his retired years. The garden occupied a total space of some 4.7 hectares (including the nine-turn bridge and the mid-pool pavilion). As time went by, it had changed hands several times and was once left deserted. In 1760 it was rebuilt with funds raised by the gentry in Shanghai and renamed the West Garden. During the early 18th century, the garden was made the offices of guilds for bean, sugar and cloth trading. It was seriously damaged during the Opium War and the Taiping Revolution. After 1949, the nine-turn bridge and the mid-pool pavilion were separated from the Yu Garden while the inner garden built in 1709 was incorporated into it. After renovation and rearrangement, the garden was restored to its former splendor and opened to the public.

The overall layout of the garden is characterized by a compact yet properly discrete arrangement and, while the structures are discrete in general, it does not in the least appear loosely set.

A series of buildings are linked up by a long zigzag corridor. Walking along the corridor, one would feel that it is leading nowhere. But turning round some pavilion or chamber, one would discover that an entirely new picture suddenly unrolls itself. Puzzled and mystified, the visitor would be surprised to find that he is back to the starting point. It is indeed a garden full of surprises and one would feel an urge to walk along a path to see what is waiting round the corner.

Inside the compound of the garden, there are about twenty to thirty pavilions, terraces, chambers, towers and halls. The Hall for Viewing the Rockery, the Pavilion for Gathering Grace, the Hall of Heralding Spring and the Hall of Enjoying the Moon are just but a few of them. The layout of these structures is such that they neither appear too closely packed nor seem too far from one another. This is one of the characteristics of gardens in South China.

The corridors in many structures are paved with bricks or tiles that form patterns of an archaic, simple but unique style. There are also green lawns, shady groves and blossoms of a thousand colors, old trees with intertwined roots as well as lakes, ponds and bridges over babbling streams. To walk among them is like entering a Chinese painting.

The Hall of Heralding Spring was once used as the headquarters of the Small Sword Society, a peasant uprising organization formed in 1853 under the leadership of Liu Lichuan and Chen Alin in response to the revolutionary movement of the Taipins. Exhibited in the hall now are some cultural relics of the Society.

In the open space to the north of the Winding Dragon Bridge which is itself a scene of the garden are three big rocks rising abruptly from the ground. Among them the one in the middle is called 'Yulinglong'. Legend has it that the rock was originally a tribute to an emperor of the Northern Song Dynasty. It is a big piece of smooth, greenish-gray limestone that resembles green jade, three meters in height, with thousands of holes, large and small. It is said that when water is poured from the top of the rock it will trickle out through one and all the holes. And if incense is burned underneath it, smoke will come out of every hole, like clouds emerging from the mountains.

Standing out in the center of the Yu Garden is a big rockery about 14 meters high, made of 2,000 tons of yellow stone quarried from the Wukang area. This

Yu Garden, with its unique arrangement of pavilions, chambers, ponds and rockeries, greatly exhibits the characteristics of gardens in South China

Yu Garden

majestic looking rockery presents a view of real mountains and forests, with overlapping peaks above the babbling streams below, giving the viewer a sense of retreat from the hustle and bustle of the city. This big rockery is the most original in style among all the Ming rockeries so far preserved south of the Changjiang.

Longhua Temple

The Longhua Temple is the oldest and largest temple in Shanghai. Built in AD. 242 during the Three Kingdoms period, it is located beside the town of Longhua to the southwest of the city.

Damaged and rebuilt several times, the present temple was put up under the reign Emperor Guang Xu in the Qing Dynasty. It has seven halls, representing the style of

Spring time, Longhua. The seven-storied pagoda could be seen from afar, indicating the location of the Longhua Temple.

The pagoda in front of the Longhua Temple

the Zen school of Buddhism which became popular in the Song Dynasty.

In front of the temple, there is a seven-storied octagonal pagoda with upturned eaves at each corner. In the past, standing on the highest point of the pagoda, one could see as far as the Huangpu River in the east and downtown Shanghai in the north. In early spring, one might enjoy a beautiful scene of peach blossoms. Formerly, Longhua was noted for its produce of flat peach and it used to be a place for outing. Since 1949 with the construction of a large number of factories and residential areas around Longhua, the outlook has been greatly changed.

In the past, when entering the gate of the temple, one would come to the Hall of Heavenly Kings (or the Maitreya Hall), then the Main Hall, with a bell tower, a drum tower and other structures on either side. The Buddhist statues looked solemn yet benign, while the eighteen arhats and the Avalokitesvara Bodhisattva assumed different forms and postures. Unfortunately, all these were ruined during the 'cultural revolution'.

At present, repairs are under way in the Longhua Temple. The work on the Maitreya Hall, the Bell Tower and the Drum Tower has already been finished and that on the Main Hall will soon be completed. Part of the sculpture of the Buddhist statue is being restored. The temple will soon be opened to the public.

Close to the Longhua Temple is the Shanghai Botanical Garden, famous for its miniature landscapes.

A Buddhist statue inside the Longhua Temple

Shanghai Botanical Garden

Formerly known as the Longhua Nursery, the botanical garden covers an area of about 66 hectares, including a portion of four hectares specially reserved as a garden of potted plants and miniature landscapes which the botanical garden is noted for.

The garden of potted plants and miniature landscapes is divided into four parts: the show room, the potted tree stumps area, and the two areas for miniature landscapes and species from outside Shanghai.

Impending structures of artificial landscapes greet the visitors at the entrance of the garden. These hills give views of soaring mountains and deep valleys ornamented with hanging waterfalls. At the center of this area are scenes of the 'pine and crane of longevity' and the 'greeting pine' which are particularly attractive.

From the artificial landscapes, a path lined with flowers on both sides leads to the show room. On the wall is a picture of the mural painting from the tomb of the Crown Prince Zhang Huai of the Tang Dynasty showing maid servants holding pots of plants. This is an evidence to show that potted landscape was already popular in China 1,200 years ago. Also displayed in the room are some aged and rare potted plants.

From the show room, a bomboo-lined winding path leads to the area of potted tree stumps. The miniature tree stumps are of different shapes and postures. Some are a hundred to several hundred years old. The pomegranate planted 240 years ago during the reign of the Qing emperor Qian Long,

Potted tree stumps in the garden of potted plants and miniature
landscape – a scene inside the Shanghai Botanical Garden

for example, is particularly noteworthy: although the greater part of its trunk has withered, the tree is still alive and may bear fruit in the harvesting season.

The pots in the miniature landscape section are only several inches in diameter. Still, they compose marvellous and spectacular scenes complete with 'mountains, rivers and luxuriant forests'.

In the section for rare plants, species from Suzhou, Fujian, Guangdong and other provinces compete in beauty and elegance.

Jade Buddha Temple

The Jade Buddha Temple is the only temple preserved in a good state and open to the public in Shanghai.

In 1882 a number of Buddhist monks and believers built a temple in Jiangwan and named it the 'Jade Buddha Temple'. The present temple on Jiangning Road, with its front gate on Anyan Road, was built in 1918.

The Jade Buddha Temple is a medium-sized temple belonging to the Zen school of Buddhism. It consists of a number of structures, such as the Heavenly King Hall, the Main Hall, the Reclining Buddha Hall and the Jade Buddha Chamber.

In the temple there are three special statues of Sakyamuni, apart from the ordinary sculptures of Buddha. The first one is a 90-cm-long jade sculpture of a reclining Sakyamuni. The other one depicts a sitting Sakyamuni, also of jade, 1.9 meters in height. Though sculptures and stone carvings of Buddha are many in China, jade Buddha statues of a large size are rare. These

The reclining Sakyamuni, one of the rare jade Buddha sculptures existing in China

two jade sculptures in the temple, therefore, are rarities of Buddhist art that attract special attention. The reclining Sakyamuni sculpture is worth particular notice since there are few reclining Buddha sculptures in China and the two in Biyun Temple and Yonghe Palace are only made of clay. The third Sakyamuni sculpture in the temple is of bronze. Also treasured in the temple is a complete volume of the *Tripitaka* (the complete Buddhist canon) printed in 1890.

Completely renovated, the Jade Buddha Temple now looks spick-and-span, with all its statues repainted. Served by monks who have returned to the temple, visitors may come to hold a Buddhist service, burn incense and pray. To serve the visitors, a vegetarian restaurant is opened.

Songjiang Square Pagoda

In the southeast of the Songjiang County which is reputed as 'Little Shanghai' is a pagoda which formerly belonged to a Xingshengjiao Temple. Now known as the Square Pagoda because of its shape, the pagoda is a nine-storied building with a height of 48.5 meters. Its construction began in the Later Han period of the Five Dynasties and was completed by the end of the 11th century during the Song Dynasty (960-1279). It was was undertaken and the pagoda was restored to its former elegance.

a thorough reconstruction was carried out. Later it fell into a dilapidated state due to lack of care. In 1975, major reconstruction was undertaken and the pagoda was restored to its former elegance.

During the reconstruction, a brick vault was discovered under the foundation of the pagoda. Dome-shaped, the vault is 65 cm long, 48 cm wide and 46 cm high. In the middle of the vault was a stone casket, on which are placed 42 coins of the Song Dynasty and a bronze Buddha in sitting posture. Inside the casket is a lacquer box wrapped in silk, already decayed. This box again contains a bronze Buddha in sleeping posture. On two sides of the casket are two silver boxes inside which are kept fossils of some animal bones symbolizing the Buddha's teeth.

The pagoda itself is built of brick and wood. Its eaves and terraces are supported by corbel brackets. Of the 177 brackets made of *nanmu* wood, 60 percent date back to the Song Dynasty. On the wall between the brackets on the third floor are two

Songjiang Square Pagoda

mural paintings of sitting Buddhas, also of
the Song period.

On the top of the pagoda is an iron
steeple. With a height of 7.85 meters, the
steeple is comprised of iron structural
members in the shapes of overturned plates,
wheels and pulleys linked together by ropes.
All these structural members are looped
through a 13-meter-long wooden pole
erected on the eighth floor of the pagoda.
The pole goes through its roof to support
the steeple, giving the pagoda a more
beautiful appearance and strengthening the
ninth story so as to make it more wind-
resistant.

Screen Wall

To the north of the Songjiang Square
Pagoda stands a large screen wall. Built in
the reign of the first emperor of Ming, the
screen wall is a rare piece of art.

The central part of the screen wall is 4.75
meters high and 6.1 meters wide. On a
surface of 30 square meters is carved a
gigantic legendary animal called *Tan*. With
a pointed horn and sharp teeth, the *Tan* is
said to be an animal with insatiable desires.
In fact, the very name *Tan* is a homophone
of the Chinese word meaning greedy. Legend
has it that after eating up all the plants and
animals in the mountains, the *Tan* goes
down to the human world to swallow gold,
silver and jewels. Yet it is still unsatisfied
and wants to swallow the rising sun from
the sea. In the end, the greedy monster is
drowned. Carved under the hoofs of the *Tan*
are precious objects like gold ingots, corals,
ruyi, jade rings, a money tree and a *lingzhi*

(heavenly medicinal herb). Alongside of all these are also carved scenes of a moralizing effect. There are the scenes of 'a carp jumping over the Dragon Gate', symbolizing promotion in status; 'a lotus blossom growing by the side of a vase with three lances', symbolizing promotion by three grades; and ' a gold seal hanging on a tree with a monkey jumping to grasp it', symbolizing the wish to be made a prince with a gold seal for this honorable post. These scenes symbolize human desires and teach the moral: avarice leads to disaster.

Zuibaichi Park

To the west of the Songjiang County is the Park of Zuibaichi. It is famous for its tablet inscriptions by ancient calligraphers and its beautiful, serene surroundings.

Confucian Temple in Jiading County

Confucian temples used to be the sacrificial halls to Confucius as well as institutions where civil examinations of county and prefectural levels were conducted. Successful scholars granted a *xiucai* degree were given the privilege to stay and study in the temples. Confucian temples were, therefore, also known as 'temple schools'.

Built in 1219 (during the Southern Song Dynasty), this Confucian Temple in Jiading was reconstructed and expanded during the Yuan, Ming and Qing dynasties. On a tablet is inscribed the essay 'History of Education in Jiading', which reads, 'The Temple School, so majestic, so imposing, attracts droves of scholars and people. The halls and courts are elegant and splendid. In nowhere else can its match be found.' Though only sixty to seventy percent of the structures have survived, what is left still captures one's admiration.

Outside the temple are three memorial arches. Called 'Yanggao' (Aiming High), 'Xingxian' (Bringing up the Virtuous), and 'Yucai' (Training the Talented), these arches were established in commemoration of the accomplishments of Confucius.

Along the arches are stone balustrades decorated with 72 stone lions in different postures. To the south of the Yanggao Arch is the Dragons Meeting Pond, where five rivers confluence to compose the scene of 'Five Dragons Embracing a Pearl'. On the east side of the Dragons Meeting Pond is the pavilion of the Kui Star, which is the star of literature.

The foremost gate of the temple, the Lingxing Gate, is decorated with a stone sculpture of fish and dragon. A fish, if fortunate enough, might transform into a dragon, so it was said. The sculpture, therefore, was a good omen to scholars passing through the gate.

A pond in the shape of a half-moon with a bridge over it lies between the Lingxing Gate and the Dacheng Gate. When the visitor crosses the bridge and comes to the Dacheng Gate, he will notice that the gate is flanked by seven stone turtles which carry on their backs stone tablets recording the history of the temple. These tablets were erected during the dynasties of Yuan, Ming and Qing.

Passing the Dacheng Gate, one would come across the Dragon-Phoenix Cypress, an old tree standing in front of the Dacheng Hall. The grand Dacheng Hall is the main hall of the temple. Formerly, a statue of Confucius with his disciples lining on both sides was enshrined in the hall. Every year, a sacrificial ceremony would be held here, following the most formal rituals, in reverence of the sage.

On the east side of the temple lies the Minglun Hall, which was used as a school or a meeting place of scholars. On the west side, a corridor of tablets boasts many invaluable inscriptions of calligraphy. These tablet inscriptions were collected here when the temple was repaired in 1959. The earliest inscription is that of the Tang Dynasty. Calligraphy inscriptions of the celebrated Confucian scholar Zhu Xi of the Song Dynasty and those of Wang Zhideng and Lou Jian of the Ming are also valuable cultural objects preserved here.

Dragons Meeting Pond
Huilong Tan

The Park of Dragons Meeting Pond was first built in 1588 (during the Ming Dynasty). Five streams feed the pond, composing a scene of 'Five Dragons Embracing a Pearl', hence the name of the pond. In the past, people used to hold dragon boat racings here on the Dragon Boat Festival (the fifth day of the fifth moon) in memory of the patriotic poet Qu Yuan. Lying in the pond is an islet called Yingkui Hill. The soaring Sky Pavilion and the nine-turn Jade Rainbow Bridge on the islet is an ideal spot for enjoying the moon and the swimming fish in the pond. At the southeast of the pond are the magnificent

Kui Star and Ancient Well pavilions.

Guyi Garden

The Guyi Garden is located in the township of Nanxiang. It was constructed in 1522-1566 during the Ming Dynasty and rebuilt in 1746 during the Qing Dynasty. Pavilions, chambers and terraces stand gracefully in the serene garden, linked together by winding paths and long corridors. Old trees shadow the flowers by a lotus pond. The Untied Boat, a pavilion in the shape of a boat, reminds the visitors of the Stone Boat of the Summer Palace in Beijing.

Songze Archaeological Site

In 1961, cultural relics were excavated near the Songze village in Qingpu County. The dating of these artifacts ranged from the Neolithic Age to the Western Zhou Dynasty. The archaeological site covers an area of several tens of thousands of square meters, comprising three layers. From the upper layer were excavated objects of the Western Zhou period. Relics of the middle layer are named the Songze culture. The lower layer had a culture similar to Majiabang's, dating back 5,800-5,900 years. It is one of the oldest historic sites of ancient civilization ever found in the Shanghai area.

Huamu Flower and Tree Nursery

The Huamu Flower and Tree Nursery, with an area of 30 hectares, is located in Huamu Commune, Chuansha County. Formerly known as the Lin's Garden, the nursery has done horticulture for more than 25 years. Rare plants are cultivated here. Trees and miniature potted plants of a great variety growing in the garden all the year round fill the air with fragrance.

Shanghai Zoo

The site of the present Shanghai Zoo was formerly a golf course built by foreigners in 1900. In 1954, it was converted into the West Suburb Park. On New Year's Day, 1980, it was renamed the Shanghai Zoo. Occupying an area of 70 hectares, the zoo is one of the most famous in China. It keeps more than 2,000 animals of 320 different species, including some rare ones that are only found in China, like the giant panda, the golden-haired monkey, the red-crowned crane, the northeastern tiger and the Changjiang aligator.

At the entrance of the zoo is a large guide map. With the help of the map, visitors can easily locate the swan lake, birds house, giant panda hill, lion and tiger hills, deer park, elephant palace, African giraff hall, and other spots, which they would like to visit.

A 15-minutes walk from the zoo is the Shanghai Exhibition Center of Agriculture, which is well worth visiting.

Historic Sites and Memorial Halls

Shanghai is a city where Mao Zedong, Zhou Enlai and Liu Shaoqi once lived and worked for the revolution. Sun Yat-sen and Soong Ching Ling also once resided in Shanghai and carried out revolutionary

Site of the First National Congress of the Communist Party of China

activities. The Communist Party of China held its first two national congresses here. Many intellectuals, too, came to Shanghai, where they wrote books and published journals. As a result, the city boasts many sites where personages in modern Chinese history left their traces. The following are descriptions of three of these places.

Site of the First National Congress of the Communist Party of China

In July 1921, representatives of Communist groups from different places in China came to Shanghai and held a congress, pronouncing the birth of the Chinese Communist Party. The meeting was attended by 13 delegates, among whom were Mao Zedong and Dong Biwu. They first met at 127 Taichang Road. Later they moved to the present building, 30 Shude Lane, Beile Road (now 76 Xingye Road).

The two-storied house was then the residence of Li Hanjun. On the first floor was Li's living room and on the second his bedroom and study. Outside there was a courtyard. The delegates held their meeting on the first floor.

The building is now converted into a museum. The setting in which the congress was held is preserved as it was. There stands in the middle of the room a dining table with a vase, cups and tea pots on its. Around the table are wooden stools. There are, against the walls, wooden chairs and tea tables, arranged as they were during the congress. On one wall now hangs the hand-writing of Dong Biwu written in February 1956, which reads, 'It is simple to start the cause, but by no means easy to carry it through.'

Lu Xun Memorial Hall

Lu Xun came to live in Shanghai in 1933 till he died in 1936. His former residence at 9 Dalu Estate, Shanyin Road, Hongkou District, is still preserved in its original state. The front room on the second floor was his bedroom and study. At the eastern end of the bedroom, there stands an iron four-poster with drapes. A bookcase is at the bedside. On the top of the bookcase are placed some decorations. By the window stand a revolving wooden chair and a desk, on which are a table lamp, an ink stone with an inkstick, a pen holder and an ash-tray. A rattan chair and a settee stand on either side of the desk. At the western end of the

'Tomb of Mr. Lu Xun' — inscription on the tomb

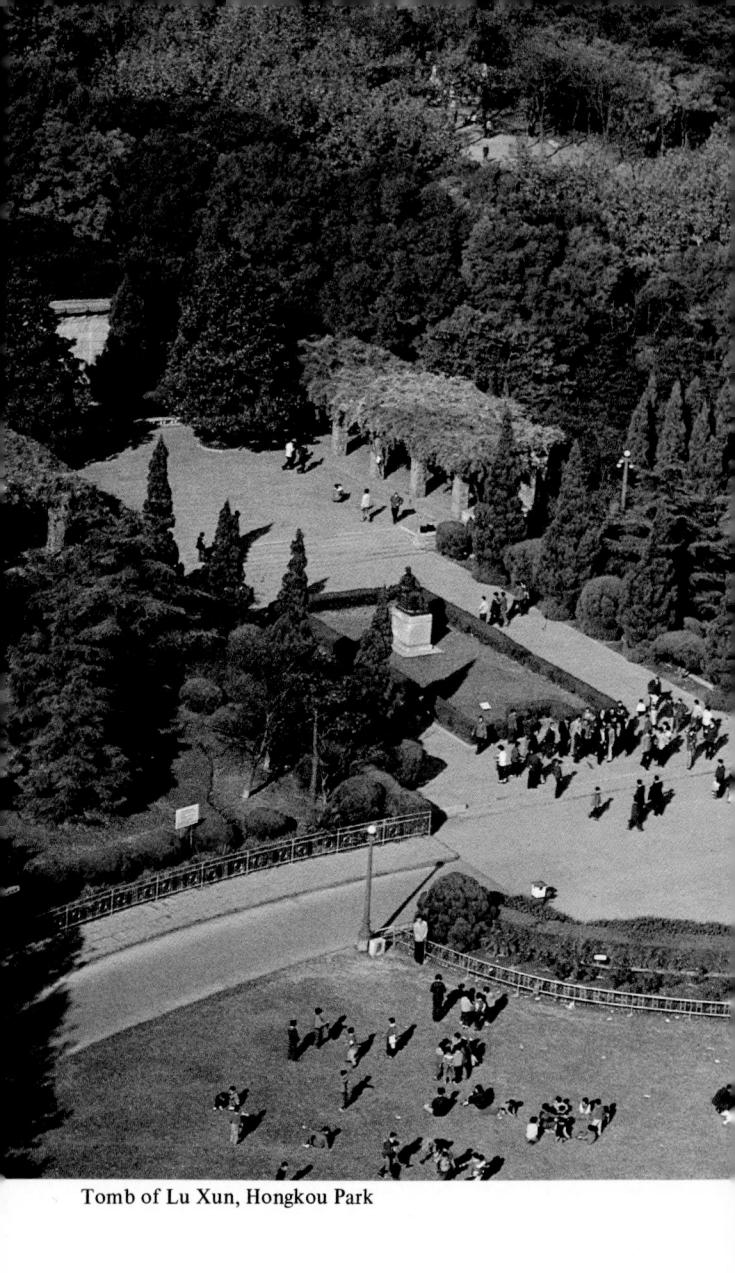

Tomb of Lu Xun, Hongkou Park

Statue of Lu Xun sitting in a rattan chair

room is a dressing table, beside which there are chairs and tea tables. The calendar on the wall shows October 19, 1936 and the little clock stops at 5:30, the time when Lu Xun died. The front room on the third floor was the bedroom of Lu Xun's son Haiying. The rear room was for guests.

The original site of the Lu Xun Memorial Hall was 10 Dalu Estate, adjoining his former residence. The present one in the Hongkou Park was set up in 1956. It consists of two floors. On display are his manuscripts, various editions of his works, books compiled by him, pictures and works of fine art.

Also moved in 1956 to the Hongkou Park is the tomb of Lu Xun. A statue of Lu Xun sitting in a rattan chair is erected in front of the tomb.

Zou Taofen Memorial Hall

In 1956, in commemoration of Zou Taofen, an outstanding journalist, political columnist and publisher, the Zou Taofen Memorial Hall was set up at 54 Lane 205 (Wanyi Fang), Chongqing Road (S), where Zou once lived and worked. His home was restored to its original state. Among the exhibits is a telegram of condolence to Zou's family sent from the Central Committee of the Chinese Communist Party in September 1944, which praised Zou for his work and announced that he was posthumously accepted as a Party member. Displayed in the hall are manuscripts written by Zou Taofen, newspapers and magazines he edited, various editions of his books, objects he used during his lifetime and words of commemoration written by national leaders.

Boat Excursion on the Huangpu River

The waterfront of the Huangpu River is lined with numerous factories, warehouses and high-rise buildings, which form a beautiful skyline. Along the banks of the river, there are 13 loading and unloading districts, more than 40 wharves and 86 buoy berths for 10,000-ton freighters. The harbor is busy all the year round with different kinds of ships shuttling in and out or anchoring in the river. A boat excursion on the river will be the best way to get a general picture of the harbor and the industries on both banks. Floating on the boat, one will see streams of barges and small motor-boats swarming the river alongside of giant ocean liners, while here and there junks of classic elegance would heave gently with the

Shanghai Harbor, an element for Shanghai to become one of the most important ports in China

Shanghai Harbor

Shanghai Harbor in the twilight: a combination of the old and the new, the romantic and the industrial

splashing waves.

Starting from the waterfront, the boat sails down the Huangpu River, where the visitors can feast their eyes on the beautiful scenes on the banks: the Huangpu Park, oldest in Shanghai, with its greenery and freshness; the Suzhou Creek with the Waibaidu Bridge spanning over it; the 22-storied Shanghai Mansions and the International Passenger Terminal; all will catch the visitors' attention. As one floats on, the flickering sparks of welders in the Shanghai Shipyard and the well-known Yangshupu Power Plant and a modern grain elevator present another face of Shanghai. Further downstream, the boat comes to Fuxing Islet — Shanghai's oldest industrial area and China's first container terminal. At the Mouth of Wusong, the ebb-and-flow water level indicator in the shape of a big clock welcomes the visitors. Further on, the famous 'sandwich water' meets the amazed visitors. Here the stream of water carried down by the Huangpu River, the silted water of the Yangtze and the sea water flow together with their colors remaining distinctively different, composing a sight of 'sandwich water'.

A boat excursion on an elegant and comfortable cruiser with all kinds of facilities is one of the best ways to know Shanghai and is most pleasurable.

China International Travel Service Shanghai Branch

Established in 1954, the Shanghai Branch of the China International Travel Service

(CITS) is connected to branches of the CITS all over China. It provides services to foreign citizens of Chinese descent and foreign tourists, businessmen, visiting scholars and journalists. Among its services are:

Providing package tours and also meeting individual traveller's needs;

Arranging boarding, lodging, transportation and city tours;

Organizing tours outside Shanghai;

Selling international through-train tickets as well as plane, train, ship and long-distance bus tickets;

Acting on tourists' behalf to apply for entry and exit visas and travel permits, to claim and check baggage, to ship goods and declare them at the customs, to pass quarantine and to make reservations for local cuisine and dinner parties;

Replying to all inquiries on travel matters.

The Shanghai Branch of the CITS has guide-interpreters who speak more than twenty languages, such as English, Japanese, French, German, Italian, Spanish, Romanian, Danish, Finnish, Greek, Korean, Thai, Burmese, Hindu, Vietnamese, Arabic, Albanian, Russian and Swahili. They are well-informed with the general facts, tourist attractions, places of interest, folktales and local customs of Shanghai, and are always ready to respond to questions and inquiries of tourists.

To enable the tourists to enjoy the best of their trip to Shanghai, special programmes of city tours are designed. Tourists joining the programmes will visit some or all of the following attractions: the Yu Garden, Guyi Garden, Songjiang Square Pagoda, Jade

Buddha Temple, Longhua Botanical Garden and the Shanghai Museum. A boat ride on the magnificent Huangpu is included in the itinerary.

Package tours of famous scenic spots like Suzhou and Hangzhou can also be arranged. Each of these tours takes a whole day.

SHOPPING

With an ample supply and good circulation of commodities in the local market, Shanghai heads the list of all the Chinese cities in industry and commerce.

Shanghai boasts a large number of stores and bazaars located all over the city. Nanjing Road, Huaihai Road, Yu Garden Bazaar and Sichuan Road are shopping centers of the city. The districts have their own shopping centers, like Jing'ansi, Xujiahui, Tilanqiao, Caojiadu, and Wujiaochang. There are, in addition, snack shops and food stores in the districts which offer round-the-clock service to customers.

The Shanghai No. 1. Department Store is the largest store in the city and in China. The Shanghai No. 10 Department Store, formerly the Wing On, ranks second. While there is no need to fully list the names of all

No. 1 Department Store, the largest of its sort in Shanghai as well as in China

Nanjing Road, one of the busiest shopping centers in Shanghai

the stores as well as the commodities they sell here, a list of the major shops can be found in Appendix I.

The following is a brief description of the specialty shops selling antiques, curios and handicrafts, which visitors may like to buy as souvenirs.

Souvenir Shopping

Shanghai Antiques and Curios Store
194-226 Guangdong Road, tel. 212292, 212864

A highly specialized shop with a long history, the store deals in antiques and curios. Traditional pottery and porcelain, green jade, jade ornaments, jewellery, ivory carvings, wood carvings, stone carvings, bronzes, pewter ware, ancient and contemporary calligraphy and paintings, ink-stones, seals, etc. are all on sale. Every item is marked with a red wax seal for export and priced according to its quality, with its date determined by specialists.

For the convenience of overseas customers, such services as money exchange and arrangement for shipment are provided in the store.

Yu Garden Bazaar
119 Yuyuan Road. tel. 289850

The Yu Garden Bazaar, with a history of over one hundred years, is well-known for its supply of small articles. The present Yu Garden Bazaar has been gradually formed through reorganizing and merging stalls and small stores that existed in the 'City God Temple' area before 1949. Comprising 122 stores, the bazaar receives on the average some 100,000 customers a day and 200,000 to 300,000 on holidays. In 1979, of all the foreign visitors to Shanghai, over 60% went to the bazaar.

The characteristics of the commodities handled by the bazaar can boil down to four words: 'small, native, special and numerous', i.e. small articles, native produce, specialty goods and numerous varieties. The bazaar handles well over 10,000 kinds of commodities. Among the specialty stores are a wig store, a bamboo ware store, a walking-stick store and a snuff bottle store. The specialized stores consist of a paper pattern store, a lace store, a lamp and lantern store and a cinnabar earthenware store. There are 50 of these in total.

Shanghai Arts and Crafts Store
190 Nanjing Road (W), tel. 535433

It is a large store in Shanghai dealing in various kinds of famous handicraft items from different parts of China.

The second floor sells articles made in Shanghai, like chests, jewellery, metal and enamel ware, pure silk embroidered wear, rugs, wollen needlepoint, hand woven or knit clothes, silk flowers, velvet birds, Hunan embroidery, ivory carvings from Guangdong, feather patchwork from Liaoning, etc.

On the third floor is an exhibition of Shanghai's arts and carfts.

In addition, the store accepts mail orders and renders such services as money exchange (including cashing of traveller's checks), packing and arrangement for shipment to all parts of the world.

Shanghai Antiques and Curios Store

Duo Yun Xuan
Nanjing Road (E)

The Duo Yun Xuan was set up in the 26th year of the reign of Emperor Guang Xu of the Qing Dynasty. With a history of over 80 years, it is a famous painting and calligraphy store in Shanghai. It deals exclusively in ancient and modern paintings, calligraphy and stone rubbings, the 'four treasures' of the study (brush, inkstick, inkstone and paper) as well as all kinds of mounting material.

The water color block prints on display are from works by renowned artists. There are beautiful ladies by Tang Yin, bamboo in black ink by Zheng Banqiao, birds and poultry by Ren Bonian, and flowers and plants by Oi Baishi. The reproductions of paintings and calligraphy made by the store keep the original expressions

Service counter of the Shanghai Arts and Crafts Store. Selected items could be packed and shipped for the customer.

Duo Yun Xuan – famous dealer in paintings and calligraphies

The 'four treasures' of the study: the brush, the ink stick, the inkstone and the paper.

and highly resemble the originals. They sell well and enjoy high popularity both in domestic and international markets.

Antique and Curio Branch of Shanghai Friendship Store
694 Nanjing Rd. (W), tel. 538092, 530975

The Antique and Curio Branch of the Shanghai Friendship Store mainly deals in various kinds of antiques and replicas. Among the articles handled are jewels, ornaments, ivory and jade carvings, calligraphy, paintings, stone rubbings, stationery (paper, brushes, inkstones and ink sticks), ceramics, embroideries, tapestries, stone, bamboo and wood carvings, bronze and enamel objects, mahogany furniture, lacquer ware, coins, seals, etc.

Every item on sale is marked with a red wax seal for export, with its date determined by specialists.

For the convenience of foreign shoppers, the store arranges for shipment, accepts mail orders and offers such service as money exchange. The store makes purchases of Chinese and foreign antiques and curios and all kinds of arts and handicrafts.

Briefly About Arts and Crafts

Gu Embroidery

Gu embroidery, a traditional handicraft of Shanghai, has a high reputation throughout the world. The origin can be traced back to the reign of Emperor Jia Jing in the Ming Dynasty, more than 400 years ago. According to one legend, a wealthy official called Gu Minshi built a garden in the north of the Shanghai County seat and named it the 'Luxiang Garden.' (The site is now on Luxiang Garden Road, Nanshi District.) He built it not only to share its beauty with his visiting friends but also to provide his female relatives with a place for doing embroidery. Some of the embroidered pieces were used in the household, others presented to friends and relatives. Of all the embroidered pieces there, the most applauded were those by the concubine of Gu's eldest son. The Buddhist figures she embroidered were exquisite in craftsmanship and true to life. Being few in number, her works were much treasured and cherished as heirlooms. The art was generally called 'Gu embroidery'. Later on, Gu's grandson and granddaughter-in-law, both adept in painting, managed to apply the theory of painting to embroidery, further promoting the traditional skill of embroidery of the Tang and Song Dynasties. The embroidered figures, landscapes, flowers and birds were vivid and colorful. As a result of steady development and improvement, Gu embroidery later became known as 'painting embroidery'. Some excellent pieces, such as 'Bathing Horse', 'Shrimps in Weeds' and so on, are now kept in the Palace Museum in Beijing and shown to visitors as best works of traditional art. As Gu's family declined later on, the females of the household made a living by selling their embroideries, which thus became commercialized. At the beginning of the Qing Dynasty, Gu's great granddaughter in her widowhood, pinched by poverty, opened a school to teach the technique of her embroidery. As a result, Gu embroidery came out of the Luxiang Garden and spread far and wide in the country with an ever increasing number of women taking up embroidery as a means of livelihood, and the embroideries, once only for decorative purposes, were put into practical use, mostly found on dresses, skirts, robes, screens and draperies. At the same time, special stores of embroidery were opened with a booming business, thus making the embroidery famous throughout South China. In the early days of the Qing Dynasty, a piece as narrow as one *chi* (about 33 cm.) in width cost several taels of silver (1 tael = 50 grams). Gu embroidery has since become a general term for Shanghai's embroidery. Even Suzhou embroidery, so well-known nowadays, can trace its origin back to Gu embroidery, as it has been developed by incorporating the technique of the latter.

Designs on Gu embroidery are based on the *tour de force* of distinguished calligraphers and painters. For the filaments, silk threads thinner than human hair are split into several or even dozens of strands. In needling, the minutest care is taken to ensure that no marks can be traced. The coloring matches that of the original. As such, the finished artifact, if mounted, might be taken for the original when the two are put side by side with each other.

New styles and techniques are now being developed. Skilled craftsmen from Songjiang county are applying Gu embroidery to articles for daily use, such as chair cushions, teapoy cloths and so on. Today, Gu embroidery enjoys a high reputation throughout the world and finds a good international market.

Woolen needle-point tapestry

The woolen needle-point work is an art of modern embroidery of Shanghai with distinctive characteristics. With threads in thousands of shade and sometimes even with several colors apiece, the artists use their rich imagination and ingenious hands to work out multi-colored pictures and patterns on grids. Every subject can be shown on the tapestry — magnificent mountains and snow-clad peaks, misty dawn scenes of the forest, kaleidoscopic clouds, mighty oceans, elegant flowers, trees, birds, grass, figures and portraits. Under a strong light, the scene on the piece will show clear layers with colors in different shades, giving a three-dimensional effect. The piece can be taken as a piece of art by itself. Such Shanghai tapestries as 'The Great Wall', 'A Hundred Flowers Competing in Beauty', 'A Distant View of Mount Qomolangma' and so on are the masterpieces unanimously commended at home and abroad. Among them, 'The Great Wall' has been displayed in a hall in the U.N. Headquarters.

Jade Carving, Ivory Carving, Lacquer Ware and Metal Handicraft

Jade carving, ivory carving, lacquer ware and metal handicraft in Shanghai are much applauded for their unique traditional style and rich local color. The following are among the masterpieces which have been made in recent years:

'A Hundred-Buddha Alms Bowl' — On a 26-cm-high alms bowl made of jade are carved symmetrically more than 90 Buddha statues with different facial expressions and postures. Several tiny Buddha images, about 1 cm in height, carved on the top of the cover, look true to life and demonstrate superb workmanship.

'Up and Down the River' — This ivory piece, carved out of a tusk of 13 cm in length, presents 16 scenic spots and historic sites along the Yellow River from its source down to its outlet to the sea. 'The Kaifeng Iron Pagoda', one of the 16 scenes, was chiselled out on a small area only 5 cm in thickness, with 6 three-dimensional layers clearly standing out. A Buddha image, as small as a little red bean housed in a pavilion, is another demonstration of exquisite craftsmanship.

'Lady Magu Presents a Birthday Gift' — It is a lacquer piece inlaid in relief. The story is based on a folk legend 'Immortals Celebrate the Birthday of the God of Longevity'. The relief work by the artisans on Magu's dress, skirt and laces gives a sense of thinness and lightness of the clothes fluttering in the breeze.

'A Hundred Dragons Playing with a Pearl' — It is a large gold ornamental work. The glass mirror modelled on the bronze mirror of the Western Han Dynasty symbolizes a pearl which is being scrambled by 10 solid dragons with moveable eyeballs and tongues and 90 dragons in relief on a gold plate. Inlaid on the circumference of the plate are precious stones like emerald, coral and agate, adding lustre to the whole piece.

The above-mentioned only describe a small portion of the 30-odd varieties of Shanghai handicrafts with local features.

CULTURAL AND LEISURE ACTIVITIES

Music, Drama and Theater

In Shanghai, there are, at present, over 40 professional performing troupes as well as dozens of performing teams, which specialize in more than ten different performing arts.

Beijing Opera

Beijing opera appeared on the stage of Shanghai a long time ago. There are now in the city three Beijing opera troupes, i.e. the Shanghai Beijing Opera Troupes N. 1, No. 2, and No. 3. They have all grown out of the former Shanghai Beijing Opera Theatre.

Shaoxing Opera, Yueju

Yueju was born in Shaoxing and Shengxian counties, Zhejiang Province, in the early 20th century. This area was once part of the state of Yue during ancient times, hence the name Yueju.

Yueju has great appeal in Shanghai. It has developed into a comprehensive art which integrates scripting, directing, acting, singing and designing. The Shanghai Yueju Troupe has successfully presented a number of historical plays and operas reflecting modern life. In its repertoire, 'Liang Shanbo and zhu Yingtai', 'A Dream of the Red Mansions', 'Story of the West Chamber' and 'Madame Xianglin' are the most well-known ones and are highly appreciated by the audience.

Kunju Opera

Kunju opera was formerly called Kunqu ballad. Being one of the earliest dramatic arts in China, it started in the Kunshan area,

Jiangsu Province. The Shanghai Kunju Opera Troupe is a major Kunju opera troupe in the country.

Shanghai Opera, Huju

Shanghai Opera a major local opera of Shanghai. In a unique artistic style created over long years of artistic practice and accumulation of experience, the performers are skilled at depicting the modern life of the farmers to the south of the Changjiang. The singing and music are exquisite, find and smooth, having a rich flavor of life.

Huai Opera, Huaiju

Huaiju was created around 200 years ago in Yancheng and Fuyang prefectures in the lower reaches of the Huai River, hence the name Huaiju. It is characterized by simplicity and naturalness. The Shanghai Huaiju Troupe was founded in 1950. Its repertoire mainly contains traditional theatrical pieces staged in ancient costumes.

Farce

Artistically unequalled in the combination of talking, mimicking, acting and singing, the local farce of Shanghai originated from monodrama and developed through absorbing various other art forms, such as Suzhou Tanhuang opera and drama. It is a special art form of comedy and farce. Employing the ingenuous plots of comedy, various local dialects and different ballad tunes, the farceurs sing praises of the good and the beautiful and condemn the bad and the ugly by artistic exaggeration, thus obtaining a humorous effect. They are adept at describing modern life.

Ping-tan Balladry

Ping-tan balladry is a name for both Suzhou story telling *(ping)* and Suzhou ballad singing *(tan)*. It is a folk art of talking and singing with a long history and is highly admired by the people. It features talking, amusing, instrument playing and singing.

Puppet Show

The Shanghai Puppet Show Troupe was founded after 1949, with the Fenglei Theater as its home base. As a result of the rapid development of puppetry in recent years, stickpuppets, which the troupe mainly uses in its performances, can move their mouths, ears, hands, legs, eyes and eyebrows freely.

Opera

The Shanghai Opera Theater is an opera company of great renown in Shanghai.

Ballet

The Shanghai Ballet Ensemble was the former No. 1 Performing Team of the Shanghai Dance School. It got its present name in the spring of 1979. Its dancers are all graduates from the Ballet Department of the Shanghai Dance School, and its orchestra musicians, graduates from the orchestra training class of the Shanghai Music Conservatory.

Folk Song and Dance

The Shanghai Song and Dance Ensemble

was formerly the No. 2 Performing Team of the Shanghai Dance School. It is composed of a performing team, an orchestra, a vocal accompaniment team and a stage designing team.

Traditional Chinese Music

The Shanghai Traditional Chinese Music Orchestra, one of the famous large orchestras in the country, was founded in 1957. In addition to giving performances, it explores new development by studying the theory of traditional music, composing modern pieces and improving musical instruments. Its music is typical of the style in the region south of the Changjiang.

Cinema

Shanghai is an important film producer in China. Apart from the Shanghai Film Studio, famous for its production of feature films, there are the Shanghai Scientific and Educational Film Studio, the Shanghai Animated Cartoon Film Studio and the Shanghai Studio for Film Translation and Dubbing.

Modern Drama

The distinguished modern drama troupes in Shanghai are the Shanghai People's Art Theater and the Shanghai Youth Modern Drama Troupe.

Acrobatics

The Shanghai Acrobatic Troupe was founded in 1951. Being one of China's famous large acrobatic troupes, it is made up of two performing teams and a circus team.

Shanghai Acrobatic Theater

The Acrobatic Troupe performing for guests inside a hotel

Recitation and Ballad Singing

The Shanghai Recitation and Ballad Singing Troupe has well-known artists who are experts at portraying the characters in various kinds of comedies, speaking different local dialects and singing many different kinds of ballads.

Symphony

The Shanghai Philharmonic Orchestra is a large well-known musical company in China and it has a group of talented composers.

Recreation Centers

Great World
1 Xizang Road (S), tel. 289760

The Great World, now called the Municipal Youth Palace, set up in 1917, used to be a multi-amusement center, the biggest of its kind in China.

Before the Great World was built, there had already been a New World, which was the oldest amusement center in old Shanghai. It was located in today's New World Department Store (opposite to the No. 1 Department Store) on the corner of present-day Nanjing Road and Xizang Road (C). The New World did a good business with large numbers of tourists. At that time, Huang Chujiu, a big speculator in Shanghai, found that running amusement centers was not only profitable but could also bring him popularity. So he bought a piece of land and built the Great World on Xixingqiao Street adjacent to the Yangjing River (at the corner of today's Xizang Road, Central and

Yan'an Road, Central). The Great World was then in the French Concession, not very far from the bustling Nanjing Road. The land was cheap and the location easily accessible. At first, the amusement center was small with only one building. But it was named the Great World in order to compete with the New World. Later, Huang Chujiu went broke and fell ill. Huang Jinrong, one of the bosses of the Shanghai underworld, took the advantage and bought the Great World and changed the name to the 'Great World of the Rongs' to make some difference from the original one. The place then became a favorite haunt of society's undesirable elements.

The Great World was taken over by the People's government on July 2, 1954, and was thoroughly transformed. In 1955, it was renamed the People's Recreation Center. The original name of the Great World was restored in 1958.

The Great World was long known as a center of amusement of great varieties. The tourists, on entering it, were immediately greeted by the distorting mirrors. In the theaters, there were performances of different local operas, such as Beijing, Shanghai, Shaoxing, Ningbo, Wuxi and Yangzhou operas, ballad singing and story telling, singing and dancing, Suzhou balladry, farce, puppet show and so on. In addition, there was a movie house, strength testing machines, rooms for games, chess, table tennis and magic show, as well as open-air concerts and acrobatics. Moreover, there were also snack shops, souvenir stores, galleries and tea-rooms, where visitors could rest and refresh themselves.

The Great World was open from 12:00 noon till night. Visitors might see several shows. One admission ticket was good for all the theaters and all the shows. The Great World was loved by the people of Shanghai. Even peasants in the suburbs and tourists from other parts of the country would all like to visit it when they came to Shanghai.

During the 'cultural revolution', however, the Great World was closed and later turned into a warehouse. Now, it has become the Shanghai Municipal Youth Palace, which still offers some of the highlights of the former Great World, such as games, acrobatics, movie shows. In addition, the Youth Palace provides training programs including music and dancing for the young people. The place is well worth visiting.

Cultural Palaces

In Shanghai, all the workers' cultural palaces and clubs offer amenities for the recreation and amusement of the working people. For example, the Shanghai Municipal Workers' Cultural Palace has reading-rooms, pingpong rooms, games rooms and tea rooms, and shows movies every day in addition to the different presentations of Suzhou balladry, modern drama, opera and so on, given by professional and amateur troupes. Another example is the Huangpu District Cultural Center, which offers similar programs to the people.

Children's Palaces

The Municipal Children's Palace, set up in 1952, is one of the first founded in China. It has 15 rooms for cultural activities, 12 for science and technology education, 10 for games, a lecture hall, a planetarium and a theater. It offers two kinds of activities for the children, namely: playground activities and training courses with terms varying from six months to two years. All children aged from 6 to 16 may participate in the activities. The enrolment for the training courses is based on personal interest, school recommendation and palace approval. Admittance to gatherings is conducted through issuing tickets. Entrance to the 'Young Friends Club' is arranged by registering with the Young Pioneers organizations of the schools, which apply to the palace. In addition, there are 12 district children's palaces and 40 neighborhood children's centers.

The 'Children's Art Theater', which has been developed from the 'Children's Theatrical Troupe', has produced a great many plays for children.

Exhibitions, Sports and Cultural Establishments

Shanghai Museum of Natural Science
260 Yan'an Rd. (E)

The Shanghai Museum of Natural Science is a five-storied building with 10,000 square meters of floor space. Set up in 1956, it now has a huge collection of specimens of plants and animals of both the past and the present. It often holds exhibitions and carries out scientific research on certain subjects. Open to the public are the following sections: paleozoology, anthropogenesis and modern zoology with specimens of insects, fishes, amphibians, reptiles, birds and mammals on display. The section of rare animals has recently begun to receive visitors.

On the first floor are displayed seven ancient human remains, including a 3,200-year-old one from Hami, in Xinjiang, and one excavated at Mawangdui, in Hunan, dating back 2,100 years. The discovery of the remains at Mawangdui has caused a great sensation throughout the world. These finds are of great value to the research into human pathology, parasitic diseases and ethnic migration. The museum is making preparations for the setting up of a planetarium and halls for paleontology, botany, anthropology and geology.

Shanghai Museum
Henan Rd. at Yan'an Rd.

The Shanghai Museum is situated on the corner of Yan'an Road and Henan Road, opposite to the Shanghai Museum of Natural Science. In 1952, the museum was opened to the public as the first art museum of its kind set up in Shanghai since the founding of the People's Republic. Its main task is to collect, keep and display cultural relics of different Chinese dynasties and do research work, compile and publish materials.

The museum consists of three exhibition halls of bronzes, ceramics and ancient Chinese paintings. It sports a magnificent collection of 106,000 objects, which were purchased by the government, supplied by other museums, donated by the people or excavated by its own staff.

On display in the bronze hall are bronzes

cast during the 17th and 14th centuries B.C. The exhibits mark the splendid civilization of ancient China and reflect the creativeness of the ancient Chinese.

Artifacts housed in the ceramic hall range from ancient crude pottery discovered in the Huanghe (Yellow River) and Changjiang basins to fine modern egg-shell porcelain. These exhibits show that ever since ancient times China has proved herself to be a country famous for her chinaware throughout the world.

Besides pottery and porcelain, ancient China was also famous for her painting and calligraphy. Drawing patterns appeared as early as the Neolithic Age while painting flourished in the Han and Tang dynasties. Displayed in the painting hall are beautiful drawing patterns, paintings, and calligraphies of different dynasties. Among the exhibits are masterpieces of celebrated ancient painters and calligraphers which comprise the treasury of human civilization.

At irregular intervals, the museum sponsors small to medium sized exhibitions, such as exhibitions of Chinese jade carving, ancient Chinese stationery, Chinese calligraphy, etc.

Shanghai Exhibition Center
1000 Yan'an Rd.

It is a comprehensive exhibition center. Built between May 4, 1954 and March 5, 1955, it covers a total area of 93,000 square meters, of which the main building occupies 32,084 square meters. The gilded tower on the top of the central hall is 106 meters high, weighing 320 tons and the decorative star atop is 3.5 meters in diameter.

The main building is made up of the central hall, the industrial hall, the east hall and the west hall. There is a theater in addition. The whole complex is magnificent with unique patterns, lighting and colors. The exhibition center has housed many foreign exhibitions, such as those by the Soviet Union, the U.S.A., Czechoslovakia, the German Democratic Republic, France, Japan, Denmark, Poland, Romania, Italy, the Federal Republic of Germany, Australia and Switzerland. Presently it also serves as a place for exchanging new technologies, products, materials and equipment. Thousands of industrial products are on display, including products of metallurgy, machine-building and electrical machinery, ship-building, chemical industry, meters and instruments, telecommunications, light industry, textiles and handicrafts.

Shanghai Exhibition Center of Agriculture
Hongqiao Rd.

Built in October, 1959, the center is located on Hongqiao Road in the west suburb of the city.

Open to the public are four sections. In the General Section are exhibited models of geographical features of the ten counties in rural Shanghai as well as photos of national model farm workers and pictures of advanced units. In the Services Section, information on the production of cotton, cereals, oil-bearing crops and over a hundred varieties of vegetables as well as statistics on animal husbandry and fishery in Shanghai is provided. The Commune and Farm

Central hall of the Shanghai Exhibition Center

Industries Section mainly introduces to the public light and textile industries as well as handicrafts in Shanghai. Here the garment processing industry is specially highlighted on. The remaining section of Science and Technology shows to visitors more than thirty kinds of scientific devices.

With its exhibits replaced once a year, the Exhibition Center of Agriculture opens from 8 a.m. to 5 p.m. Monday through Saturday (except Saturday afternoon).

Shanghai Indoor Stadium
Zhongshan Rd. (S2)

A modern stadium in a unique and novel style, it has a total building space of 47,000 square meters, of which the competition hall occupies 31,000 square meters and rises as high as a ten-storied building. The stadium has a seating capacity of 18,000, hence the name 'ten-thousand-spectator stadium'. There is not a single column in the circular hall, which is 22 meters high and 110 meters in diameter.

The stadium is not only home to national and international ball games and gymnastic, weight lifting and fencing competitions, but also the ground for holding mass rallies, concerts, and other popular entertainments.

Shanghai Municipal Library
325 Nanjing Rd. (W)

Set up in 1952, it now comprises four specialized libraries: the Science and Technology Library, the Historical Document Library, the Periodical and News-paper Library, and the Children's Library. With a collection of 7 million volumes of books, including 150,000 rare books, 14,000 kinds of Chinese and foreign periodicals and more than 300 kinds of Chinese and foreign newspapers, it is the second largest library in China.

Among its collections are Chinese and foreign documents, books and materials of the past and the present, such as precious revolutionary documents, fine block-printed editions of handwritten copies and manuscripts of the Song, Yuan, Ming and Qing dynasties, which are considered a rare national cultural heritage.

The library has also a complete collection of all the issues of *Shen Bao (Shanghai Newspaper)* from the time when it was first published in 1872 till 1949, with a total of 77 years, and a complete collection of the *North China Daily News* from the first issue in 1864 to the last in 1950, 86 years in all. As well, it has a complete collection of the *Digest of American Chemistry* from 1907 up to now, the *German Chemical Journal* from 1868 up to this day and the *Journal of the Janapese Chemical Institute* from 1926 to the present. Records, tapes, microfilms and metal and stone rubbings are also collected.

The library often sponsors various exhibitions and gives guidance to readers. Service hours are from 8:30 a.m. to 8:00 p.m. every day.

Publishers and Bookstores

With an annual publication of 1,700 titles of books which amount to 11% of the nation's total publication, Shanghai ranks second to Beijing in publication in China. At present, there are 15 publishing houses, with a staff of 1,800 editors and workers.

Bookstores can be found all over Shanghai. Among the major ones the following may be of special interest to the tourist:

Foreign Languages Bookstore (Waiwen shudian)
390 Fuzhou Rd

The bookstore not only sells books and publications in foreign languages, but also holds exhibitions of books in foreign languages.

Duo Yun Xuan
422 Nanjing Rd. (E)

This is the sales department of the Shanghai Painting and Calligraphy Society. It mainly sells ancient and modern Chinese paintings and calligraphies, traditional watercolor block prints, tablet calligraphy rubbings, engraved stone seals, brushes, inkstones, paper and inksticks, etc. (see also page 92)

Guji (Chi. Classics) Bookstore
424 Fuzhou Rd

It specializes in the selling of ancient books published in olden days and ancient works of literature and history published in modern times.

Xinhua (New China) Bookstores

Branches and sales departments (totalling 94) of the Shanghai Municipal Xinhua Bookstore can be found in every district and county. In addition, 45 bookstalls are set up in large factories, schools and crowded streets.

APPENDICES

Directory

N.B. This directory only includes major or representative companies or institutions, and is by no means an exhaustive list.

AIRLINES 航空

Cathay Pacific Airways 國泰航空公司
Room 123, Jingjiang Hotel 377899

Civil Aviation Administration of China (CAAC), Shanghai 中國民航
789 Yan'an Rd. (C)   International   532255
                        Domestic   535953

Hongqiao Airport, inquiries
虹橋飛機場問訊處 537664

Japan Air Lines 日本航空公司
1202 Huaihai Rd. (C) 378467

Pan American World Airways 泛美航空公司
Room 103, Jing'an Guest House 530210

ANTIQUES, ARTS AND CRAFTS
古董・工藝品

Antique and Curio Branch of the Friendship Store 友誼商店古玩分店
694 Nanjing Rd. (W) 530975

Duo Yun Xuan 朵雲軒
422 Nanjing Rd. (E) 223784

Shanghai Antiques and Curios Store 上海文物商店
194-226 Guangdong Rd. 212292
                                          212864

Shanghai Arts and Crafts Store
190 Nanjing Rd. (W) 上海工藝品 535433

Yuhua Arts and Crafts Store
933 Huaihai Rd. (C) 玉華工藝商店 374779

BANKS 銀行

Bank of China, Shanghai Branch 中國銀行
23 Zhongshan Rd. (EI)   217466

Hongkong & Shanghai Banking
Corporation 滙豐銀行
185 Yuanmingyuan Rd.   218383

BOOKSTORES 書店

Children's Bookstore 少年兒童書店
772 Nanjing Rd. (W)   533467

Chinese Classics Bookstore 古籍書店
424 Fuzhou Rd.   224984

Foreign Languages Bookstore 外文書店
390 Fuzhou Rd.   224109

Music Bookstore 音樂書店
365 Xizang Rd. (C)   223213

Shanghai Bookstore 上海書店
401 Fuzhou Rd.   282894

Shanghai Scientific & Technological
Bookstore 上海科技書店
221 Henan Rd. (C)   212766

Xinhua Bookstore 新華書店
345 Nanjing Rd. (E)   222668
771 Nanjing Rd. (W)   533053

CLUBS 俱樂部

International Club 國際俱樂部
63 Yan'an Rd. (W)   538513

International Seamen's Club 國際海員俱樂部
20 Huangpu Rd.   244204

Jinjiang Club 錦江俱樂部
58 Maoming Rd. (S)   370115

COMMUNICATIONS 通訊

Long Distance Calls 長途電話
Domestic   113
International   565956

Long Distance Telephone Office 長途電話局
1761 Sichuan Rd. (N)   660400

Telegraph Office, Business Dept. 電報局
30 Nanjing Rd. (E)   210022

CONSULATES 領事館

French Consulate General 法國領事館
1431 Huaihai Rd. (C)   377414

Japanese Consulate General 日本領事館
1517 Huaihai Rd. (C)   372073

Polish Consulate General 波蘭領事館
618 Jianguo Rd. (W)   370952

U.S. Consulate General 美國領事館
1469 Huaihai Rd. (C)   379880

DEPARTMENT STORES AND OTHER SHOPS 商店

China Stamp Collection Co.,
Shanghai Office 中國郵票公司
244 Nanjing Rd. (E)   214276

Friendship Store 友誼商店
33 Zhongshan Rd. (EI)   219698

Guanlong Photographic Supplies
冠龍照相材料商店
180 Nanjing Rd. (E)   214015

Old Zhouhuchen's Brushes 老周虎臣筆墨店
90 Henan Rd. (C)

Overseas Chinese Store 華僑商店
627 Nanjing Rd. (E)   225424

Shanghai No. 1 Department Store
第一百貨商店
830 Nanjing Rd. (E)   223344

Shanghai No. 2 Department Store
第二百貨商店
889 Huaihai Rd. (C)   374424

Shanghai No. 10 Department Store
第十百貨商店
635 Nanjing Rd. (E)   224466

Shanghai No. 1 Drug Store 第一醫藥商店
614 Nanjing Rd. (E)   224567

Shanghai Flower & Bird Store 上海花鳥商店
364 Nanjing Rd. (W)   535483

Shanghai Musical Instruments Mfg.,
Sales Dept. 上海民族樂器廠服務部
114 Nanjing Rd. (E)   213869

Wangkai Photo Studio 王開照相館
378 Nanjing Rd. (E)   521098

Wangxingji Fan Store 王星記扇莊
782 Nanjing Rd. (E)   224684

Yu Garden Bazaar 豫園商場
119 Yuyuan Rd.   289850

Zhangxiaoquan Knife & Scissors Store
張小泉刀剪商店
490 Nanjing Rd. (E)   223858

FABRIC, GARMENT & WEAR STORES
服裝店

Laojiefu Woolen & Silk Fabric
Store 老介福呢絨綢緞商店
257 Nanjing Rd. (E)   219292

Shanghai Silk Fabric Store 上海綢緞商店
592 Nanjing Rd. (E)   224830

Shanghai Sports Goods Store 上海體育用品商店
160 Nanjing Rd. (E)   218863

Shanghai Women's Article Store
上海市婦女用品商店
451-475 Huaihai Rd. (C)   285999

Xiangyang Children's Article Store
向陽兒童用品商店
993 Nanjing Rd. (W)   562422

Xinshijie Garment Store 新世界服裝商店
798-806 Huaihai Rd. (C)   373620

Zhonghua Leather Shoe Store 中華皮鞋店
252 Nanjing Rd. (E)   212769

FOODSTUFFS STORES AND BAKERIES 食品

Harbin Bakery & Confectionery 哈爾濱食品廠
919 Huaihai Rd. (C)   371013

Kaige Bakery & Confectionery,
Sales Dept. 凱歌食品店
1001 Nanjing Rd. (W)   535007

Laodachang Bakery & Confectionery,
Sales Dept. 老大昌
377 Huaihai Rd. (C)   374745

Sanyan South-China Delicacies
Store 三陽南貨店
630 Nanjing Rd. (E)   223353

Shanghai Bakery 上海食品廠
975 Huaihai Rd. (C)   376142

Shanghai No. 1 Foodstuffs Store
上海第一食品商店
720 Nanjing Rd. (E)   222777

EXHIBITIONS, CULTURAL AND SPORTS ESTABLISHMENTS
展覽館、文化館

Shanghai Exhbn. Center of Agric. 農業展覽館
2270 Hongqiao Rd.   329588

Shanghai Art Gallery
456 Nanjing Rd. (W)   532684

Shanghai Exhibition Center 上海展覽館
1000 Yan'an Rd. (C)   563037

Shanghai Indoor Stadium 上海體育館
1111 Caoxi Rd. (N)   393966

Shanghai Municipal Children's
Palace 上海市少年宮
64 Yan'an Rd. (W)   525537

Shanghai Municipal Library 上海圖書館
325 Nanjing Rd. (W)   563176

Shanghai Municipal Worker's
Cultural Palace 上海市工人文化宮
120 Xizang Rd. (C)   226155

Shanghai Municipal Youth Palace
上海市青年宮
1 Xizang Rd. (S)   289760

Shanghai Museum 上海博物館
16 Henan Rd. (S)   380160

Shanghai Museum of Natural
Science 上海自然博物館
260 Yan'an Rd. (E)   213548

HOTELS 酒店

Dahua Guest House 達華賓館
914 Yan'an Rd. (W)   532079

Hengshan Guest House 衡山賓館
534 Hengshan Rd.   377050

Jing'an Guest House 靜安賓館
370 Huashan Rd.   563050

Jinjiang Hotel 錦江飯店
59 Maoming Rd. (S)   534242

Overseas Chinese Hotel 華僑飯店
104 Nanjing Rd. (W)   226226

Park Hotel 國際飯店
170 Nanjing Rd. (W)   225225

Peace Hotel 和平飯店
20 Nanjing Rd. (E)   211244

Shanghai Mansions 上海大厦
20 Suzhou Rd. (N)   246260

PARKS 公園

Caoxi Park 漕溪公園
203 Caoxi Rd.   280513

Changfeng Park 長風公園
25 Daduhe Rd.   577355

Fuxing Park 復興公園
105 Yandang Rd.   283296

Guilin Park 桂林公園
1 Guilin Rd.   380042

Hongkou Park 虹口公園
146 Jiangwan Rd.   662894

Huangpu Park 黄浦公園
The Bund   214619

Longhua Park 龍華公園
2878 Longhua Rd.   380581

People's Park 人民公園
231 Nanjing Rd. (W)   532875

Shanghai Botanical Garden 上海植物園
1 Baishe Rd.   389413

Shanghai Zoo 上海動物園
2381 Hongqiao Rd.   329775

Zhongshan Park 中山公園
780 Changning Rd.   521478

PLACES OF INTEREST 主要遊覽點

Confucian Temple in Jiading 孔廟
West Gate, Jiading County Seat

Former Residence of Zhou Enlai 周公館
107 Sinan Rd.

Guyi Garden 古漪園
Nanxiang, Jiading County   951478

Huayan Pagoda 華嚴塔
Songyin, Jinshan County

Jade Buddha Temple 玉佛寺
170 Anyuan Rd.   538805

Longhua Temple and Longhua
Pagoda 龍華寺、龍華塔
Longhua, Shanghai County   389997

Lu Xun Memorial Hall
魯迅紀念館
Hongkou Park, 146 Jiangwan Rd.

Old Temple of Zhenru 眞如寺
Zhenru, Jiading County

Qushui Garden 曲水園
Zhongshan Park, Qingpu County

Site of the First National Party
Congress 中共一大會址
76 Xinye Rd.   281177

Songjiang Square Pagoda 松江方塔
Southeast of Songjiang County Seat   228228

Songze Archaeological Site 崧澤遺址
Songze Production Brigade, Qingpu County

Tomb of Madame Soong Ching
Ling 宋慶齡墓
International Cemetery

Tomb of Xu Guangqi 徐光啓墓
Nandan Park, Xujiahui, Xuhui District

Yu Garden 豫園
132 Anren St.   283251

Zou Taofen Memorial Hall 韜奮紀念館
53, Lane 205, Chongqing Rd. (S)   282811

RESTAURANTS 菜館

Chengdu Restaurant 成都飯店
795 Huaihai Rd. (C)   376412

Datong Restaurant 大同酒家
725 Huaihai Rd. (C)   378317

Deda Western Food Restaurant
德大西菜社
359 Sichuan Rd. (C)   213810

Dongfeng Hotel Restaurant 東風飯店
3 Zhongshan Rd. (1)   218060

Gongdelin Vegetarian Restaurant
43 Huanghe Rd. 功德林素食處   531313

Great Fortune Restaurant 大鴻運酒樓
Dahongyun Jiulou
556 Fuzhou Rd.   223176

Jade Buddha Temple Vegetarian
Restaurant 玉佛寺素齋
170 Anyuan Rd.   535745

Luyangcun Restaurant 綠楊邨酒家
763 Nanjing Rd. (W)   532721

Meilongzhen Restaurant 梅龍鎮酒家
1082 Nanjing Rd. (W)   562718

Meixin Restaurant 美心酒家
316 Shaanxi Rd. (S)   373991

Muslim Restaurant 清真飯店
710 Fuzhou Rd.   224876

Nanjing Restaurant 南京飯店
200 Shanxi Rd. (S)   221455

People's Restaurant 人民飯店
226 Nanjing Rd. (W)   537351

The Red House 紅房子西菜館
37 Shaanxi Rd. (S)   565748

Shanghai Old Town Restaurant 上海老飯店
242 Fuyou Rd.   282782

Sichuan Restaurant 四川飯店
457 Nanjing Rd. (E)   221965

Xinghualou Restaurant 杏花樓
343 Fuzhou Rd.   282747

Xinya Guangzhou Restaurant 新雅粵菜館
719 Nanjing Rd. (E)   224393

Yangzhou Restaurant 揚州飯店
457 Nanjing Rd. (E)   222779

Yanyunlou Restaurant 燕雲樓
755 Nanjing Rd. (E)   223293

Yueyanglou Restaurant 岳陽樓
28 Xizang Rd. (S)   282670

THEATERS AND CINEMAS 劇場，電影院

Children's Art Theater 兒童藝術劇場
555 Yan'an Rd. (C)   537171

East Lake Cinema 東湖電影院
9 Donghu Rd.   373612

Da Guang Ming Cinema 大光明電影院
216 Nanjing Rd. (W)   532223

Great Shanghai Cinema 大上海電影院
500 Xizang Rd. (C)   293322

Guotai Cinema 國泰電影院
870 Huaihai Rd. (C)   373757

People's Grand Theater 人民大舞台
663 Jiujiang Rd.   224473

Shanghai Acrobatic Theater 上海雜技場
400 Nanjing Rd. (W)   564051

Shanghai Art Theater 上海藝術劇場
57 Maoming Rd. (S)   564631

Shanghai Concert Hall 上海音樂廳
523 Yan'an Rd. (E)   281714

Shanghai Cultural Square 上海文化廣場
36 Yongjia Rd.   377170

TRANSPORT 交通

Rented Cars 出租汽車

Limousines and mini-buses	564444
Buses	215555
Three-wheelers	213090

Shanghai Friendship Taxi/Bus Co.
上海友誼汽車服務公司

Dahua Guest House	523079
Hengshan Guest House	377050
Jing'an Guest House	563050
Jinjiang Hotel	534242
Overseas Chinese Hotel	226226
Peace Hotel	211244-281
Shanghai Mansions	246260-209

Shanghai Railway North Station
上海火車北站

Inquiries	242299

MISCELLANEOUS 其他

China Council for Promotion of International Trade 中國國際貿易促進委員會
27 Zhongshan Rd. (EI)   214244

China International Travel Service, Shanghai Branch 中國國際旅行社
59 Xianggang Rd.   217200

People's Insurance Company of China 中國人民保險公司
23 Zhongshan Rd. (EI)   217466

How to Pronounce the Chinese Phonetic Alphabets

All Chinese personal and place names in the book are transcribed in the *Hanyu pinyin* system, as the system is now used in China. The Chinese phrases in Appendix III are also accompanied by their transcriptions in *pinyin*. For the benefit of those who are not familiar with the system, we have listed in the following the Chinese phonetic alphabets in *pinyin*, followed by their equivalents in the Wade system and brief descriptions which draw examples from English words.

'a'	(a),	a vowel, as in far;
'b'	(p),	a consonant, as in be;
'c'	(ts'),	a consonant, as 'ts' in its;
'ch'	(ch'),	a consonant, as 'ch' in church, strongly aspirated;
'd'	(t),	a consonant, as in do;
'e'	(e),	a vowel, as 'er' in her, the 'r' being silent; but 'ie', a diphthong, as in yes and 'ei', a diphthong, as in way;
'f'	(f),	a consonant, as in foot;
'g'	(k),	a consonant, as in go;
'h'	(h),	a consonant, as in her, strongly aspirated;
'i'	(i),	a vowel, two prounciations: 1. as in eat 2. as in sir in syllables beginning with the consonants c, ch, r, s, sh, z and zh;

'j'	(ch),	a consonant, as in jeep;
'k'	(k'),	a consonant, as in kind, strongly aspirated;
'l'	(l),	a consonant, as in land;
'm'	(m),	a consonant, as in me;
'n'	(n),	a consonant, as in no;
'o'	(o),	a vowel, as 'aw' in law;
'p'	(p'),	a consonant, as in par, strongly aspirated;
'q'	(ch'),	a consonant, as 'ch' in cheek;
'r'	(j),	a consonant pronounced as 'r' but not rolled, or like 'z' in azure;
's'	(s, ss, sz),	a consonant, as in sister;
'sh'	(sh),	a consonant, as 'sh' in shore;
't'	(t'),	a consonant, as in top, strongly aspirated;
'u'	(u)	a vowel, as in too; and a vowel, as in the
'ü'	(u)	French 'u' in 'tu' or the German umlauted 'u' in 'Muenchen';
'v'	(v),	is used only to produce foreign and national minority words, and local dialects;
'w'	(w),	used as a semi-vowel in syllables beginning with 'u' when not preceded by consonants, pronounced as in want;
'x'	(hs),	a consonant, as 'sh' in she;
'y'	(y),	used as a semi-vowel in syllables beginning with 'i' or 'u' when not preceded by consonants, pronounced as in yet;

'z'   (ts, tz),   a consonant, as in zero;
'zh'   (ch),   a consonant, as 'j' in jump.

In Chinese, a character may be spoken in four different tones, namely, the level tone, the rising tone, the falling - rising tone and the falling tone. Different tones of a character convey different meanings. In the *Hanyu pinyin*, the tones are denoted by different forms of strokes placed above the active vowel. These are (taking 'a' for example):

ā,   level;
á,   rising;
ǎ,   falling-rising; and
à,   falling.

In some cases, such syllables as 'er' and 'zi' will not be marked by any strokes. Such a syllable is what we call an unstressed syllable and is pronounced without its original pitch. The tone of such a syllable is known as the light tone, a tone in addition to the four basic types mentioned above.

Chinese Phrases for Visitors

In this table the English phrases are arranged alphabetically. Following them are the romanizations of their Chinese equivalents, accompanied by Chinese characters.

afternoon
    xià wǔ 下午

airport, Hongqiao Airport
    fēi jī chǎng, hóng qiáo jī chǎng
    飛機塲，虹橋機塲

apple
    píng gǔo 蘋果

banana
    xiāng jiāo 香蕉

beer
    pí jiǔ 啤酒

'Bottoms up!'
    gān bēi 乾杯

bowl
    wǎn 碗

breakfast
    zǎo fàn 早飯

bus
    gōng gòng qì chē 公共汽車

bus stop
    qì chē zhàn 汽車站

(very) cheap
    (hěn) pián yi（很）便宜

China
    zhōng gúo 中國

China International Travel Service
    zhōng gúo gúo jì lǚ xíng shè 中國國際旅行社

Chinese
    zhōng gúo rén 中國人

Chinese meal
    zhōng cān 中餐

coca cola
    kě kǒu kě lè 可口可樂

cold
    lěng 冷

comrade
    tóng zhì 同志

delicious
    hǎo chī 好吃

department store
    bǎi huò shāng diàn 百貨商店

dinner
    wǎn fàn 晚飯

egg
    jī dàn 鶏蛋

evening
    wǎn shàng 晚上

(too) expensive
    (tài) guì (太)貴

film
    diàn yǐng 電影

to watch a film
    kàn diàn yǐng 看電影

fork
　　chā zi 叉子

friend(s)
　　péng yǒu (men) 朋友（們）

friendship
　　yǒu yì 友誼

Friendship Store
　　yǒu yì shāng diàn 友誼商店

good-bye
　　zài jiàn 再見

good morning
　　zǎo shàng hǎo 早上好

good evening
　　wǎn shàng hǎo 晚上好

good night
　　wǎn ān 晚安

guest house, hotel
　　bīn guǎn, lǚ guǎn 賓館，旅館

he, him (they, them)
　　tā (tā men) 他（他們）

hot (temperature)
　　rè 熱

hot (taste)
　　là 辣

"How are you?"
　　ní hǎo mā? "你好嗎？"

"How do you do."
　　ní hǎo "你好！"

"How much is this?"
　　zhè gè duō shǎo qián? "這個多少錢？"

I, me
　　wǒ 我

ice cream
　　bīng qī lín 冰淇淋

ice cube
　　bīng kuài 冰塊

key
　　yào shi 鎖匙

knife
　　dāo zi 刀子

lemon soda
　　níng méng shuǐ 檸檬水

lunch
　　zhōng fàn 中飯

man
　　nán rén 男人

milk
　　niú nǎi 牛奶

mineral water
　　kuàng quán shuǐ 礦泉水

Miss (Yang)
　　(yáng) xiǎo jiě （楊）小姐

Mr. (Yang)
　　(yáng) xiān shēng （楊）先生

Mrs. (Yang)
　　(yáng) tài tài （楊）太太

morning
　　shàng wǔ 上午

no
　　bù 不

orange
jú zǐ 桔子

park
gōng yuán 公園

plate
dié zi 碟子

please
qǐng 請

railway station
huǒ chē zhàn 火車站

restaurant
cān tīng 餐廳

room
fáng jian 房間

(a) seat
(yī gè) zuò wèi （一個）座位

Shanghai
shàng hǎi 上海

Shanghailander
shàng hǎi rén 上海人

Shanghai North Station
shàng hǎi běi zhàn 上海北站

"Sorry!"
duì bù qǐ "對不起！"

soup
tāng 湯

spoon
tiáo gēng 調羹

store
shāng diàn 商店

sugar
  táng 糖

table
  zhuo zi 桌子

taxi
  chū zū qì chē 出租汽車

tea
  chá 茶

"Thank you!"
  xiè xiè nǐ "謝謝你！"

time
  shí jiàn 時間

"What time is it?"
  xiàn zài jǐ diǎn? "現在幾點？"

toast
  tǔ sī 吐司

today
  jīn tiān 今天

toilet
  cè suǒ 廁所

ladies' room
  nǚ cè suǒ 女廁所

men's room
  nán cè suǒ 男廁所

tomorrow
  míng tiān 明天

tourist
  lǚ kè 旅客

train
  huǒ chē 火車

trolley-bus
　wú guǐ diàn chē 無軌電車

No. (11) trolley-bus
　(shí yī) lù diàn chē （十一）路電車

very good (very well)
　hěn hǎo 很好

we, us
　wǒ mén 我們

welcome
　huān yíng 歡迎

western meal
　xī cān 西餐

woman
　nǚ rén 女人

yes
　shì de 是的

yesterday
　zuó tiān 昨天

you
　nǐ (*pl.* nǐ men) 你（你們）

zoo
　dòng wù yuán 動物園

The directions
　fāng xiàng 方向

　east
　　dōng 東

　west
　　xī 西

　north
　　běi 北

south
 nán 南

left
 zuǒ 左

right
 yòu 右

go straight
 xiàng qián zǒu 向前走

turn right
 xiàng yòu zhuan 向右轉

The numbers
 shù zì 數字

 one
  yī 一

 two
  èr 二

 three
  sān 三

 four
  sì 四

 five
  wǔ 五

 six
  liù 六

 seven
  qī 七

 eight
  bā 八

 nine
  jiǔ 九

ten
　　shí 十

eleven
　　shí yī 十一

twenty
　　èr shí 二十

twenty-one
　　èr shí yī 二十一

one hundred
　　yī bǎi 一百

one thousand
　　yī qiān 一千

ten thousand
　　yī wàn 一萬

The four seasons
　　sì jì 四季

spring
　　chūn tiān 春天

summer
　　xià tiān 夏天

autumn
　　qiū tiān 秋天

winter
　　dōng tiān 冬天

The date
　　rì qī 日期

year
　　nián 年

month
　　yuè 月

January
  yī yuè 一月

February
  èr yuè 二月

November
  shí yī yuè 十一月

December
  shí èr yuè 十二月

25th December
  shí èr yuè èr shí wǔ hào
  十二月二十五號

1st January, 1983
  yī jiǔ bā sān nián yī yuè yī hào
  一九八三年一月一號

The currency
  huò bì 貨幣

RMB
  rén mín bì 人民幣

dollar
  yuán 圓，元

cents
  fēn 分

one dollar
  yī yuán 壹圓

ten cents
  yī jiǎo 壹角

one cent
  yī fēn 壹分

RMB ¥4.55
  sī yuán wǔ jiǎo wǔ fēn
  肆圓伍角伍分

Chronology of Chinese Dynasties

Xia	c. 21st-16th century B.C.
Shang	c. 16th-11th century B.C.
Western Zhou	c. 11th century to 771 B.C.
Eastern Zhou	770-256 B.C.
Spring and Autumn Period	770-476 B.C.
Warring States	475-221 B.C.
Qin	221-207 B.C.
Western Han	206 B.C.-A.D. 24
Eastern Han	25-220
Three Kingdoms	220-280
Wei	220-265
Shu	221-263
Wu	222-280
Western Jin	265-316
Eastern Jin	317-420
Southern and Northern Dynasties	420-589
Southern Dynasties	
Song	420-479
Qi	479-502
Liang	502-557
Chen	557-589
Northern Dynasties	
Northern Wei	386-534
Eastern Wei	534-550
Western Wei	535-556
Northern Qi	550-577
Northern Zhou	557-581
Sui	581-618
Tang	618-907
Five Dynasties	907-960
Later Liang	907-923
Later Tang	923-936

Later Jin	936-946
Later Han	947-950
Later Zhou	951-960
Northern Song	960-1127
Liao	916-1125
Jin	1115-1234
Southern Song	1127-1279
Yuan	1271-1368
Ming	1368-1644
Qing	1644-1911
Republic	1912-1949
People's Republic	established 1949

OTHER JOINT TITLES ON CHINA TRAVELS

In Search of Old Nanking
by Barry Till
with the assistance of Paula Swart

paperback HK$25.00
210 × 135mm 241 pages
100 illustrations
ISBN 962·04·0112·3

This intends not only to serve as a detailed guide for
the tourist visiting Nanking, but also hopes to offer a
new insight into the history of the city. The book
briefly outlines the history of the city and carefully
catalogues and describes the more than one hundred
historical sites found in the city. It deals not only
with the most famous historical sites but also with
lesser known ancient sites that nevertheless are also
of historical importance. The many stories and
legends attached to these historical sites have also
been included in this study. The book further
contains photographs, illustrations and stone
rubbings which help to examine deeper into the
significance of the historical relics.

In Search of Old Shanghai
by Pan Ling

paperback HK$25.00
210 × 135mm 144 pages
80 illustrations
ISBN 962·04·0195·6

Known as a 'paradise of adventurers', Shanghai had everything you could expect — the millionaire and the coolie, the mobster and the revolutionary, the singsong girl and the poet. Here property tycoons like Silas Hardoon and Victor Sassoon made their fortunes; here a waterfront urchin named Du Yuesheng rose to become the Al Capone of China; here a movie starlet named Jiang Qing, one day to become Madame Mao, hankered after success on the silver screen; here Mao Zedong himself came one day to help found the Chinese Community Party.

This book, seeking the traces these people have left in the streets and buildings of present-day Shanghai, acts as a guide to that lost world. It will appeal specially to the visitor, jogging the memory of those who knew the city, and showing those who don't the way to knowing it better.